ISLAY

PEVENSEY ISLAND GUIDES

ISLAY

Norman Newton

David and Charles

A DAVID & CHARLES BOOK
Copyright © David & Charles Limited
1995, 1997, 2001, 2003, 2005,
2006, 2009

David & Charles is an imprint
of F&W Media International, Ltd
Brunel House, Forde Close,
Newton Abbot, TQ12 4PU, UK

F&W Media International, Ltd
is a subsidiary of F+W Media, Inc
10151 Carver Road, Suite #200,
Blue Ash, OH 45242, USA

First published in the UK in 1995
Reprinted 1997, 2001, 2003, 2005,
2006, 2009, 2011, 2012

A catalogue record for this book is
available from the British Library.

ISBN-13: 978-0-7153-3495-9 paperback
ISBN-10: 0-7153-3495-6 paperback

Printed in China by WKT
Company Limited
for David & Charles
Brunel House   Newton Abbot   Devon

David & Charles publish high quality
books on a wide range of subjects.
For more great book ideas visit:
www.rubooks.co.uk

CONTENTS

Title page: From near Dun Bhoraraig looking south-east over the Sound of Islay

Half-title: Grave slab in Kildalton church

Left: Paps of Jura near Bunnahabhainn

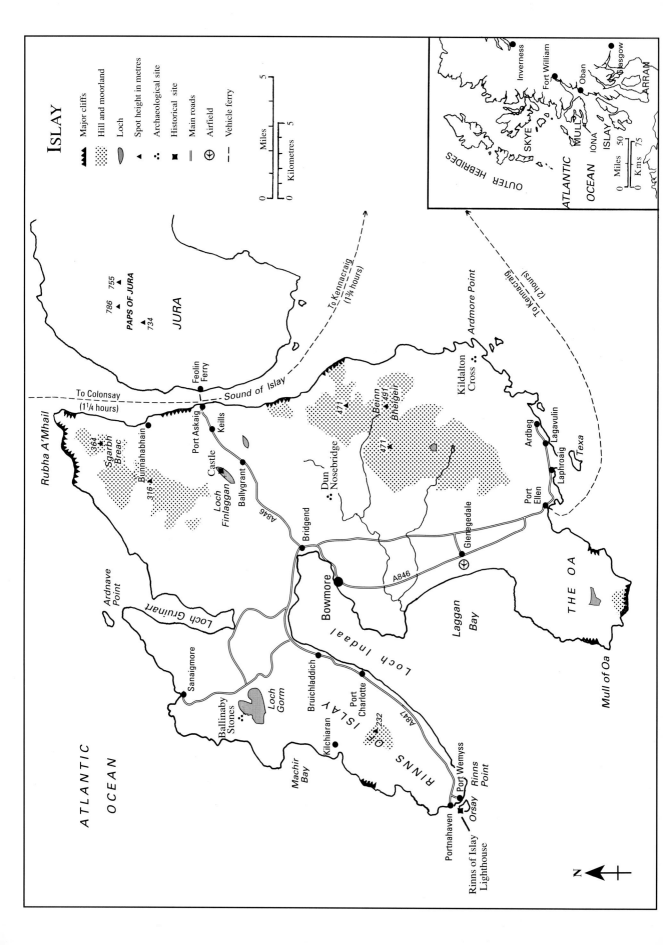

INTRODUCTION

THIS BOOK is a guide to the Hebridean island of Islay, an introduction for visitors, guaranteed to whet your appetite and make your visit more interesting and more rewarding.

Islay is a mixture of landscapes and cultural and historical influences. The underlying rocks are the result of one part of the earth's crust shearing off from another, leaving rocks of different periods side by side in the geological record. In a strange way, human history on Islay has been similarly turbulent, as first one culture and then another arrived on the island, clashed with its inhabitants in an often violent eruption of blood-letting, before things settled down – until the next invasion.

As a Hebridean society at the end of the twentieth century, Islay has a lot going for it, though it's not without its problems. It's a beautiful place, with stunning landscapes and seascapes, miles of sandy beaches, rugged hills, pleasing farmland and sheltered woods. In this book we guide you through the whole island, district by district, pausing from time to time to give some background information on the history, wildlife, mountains, climate, natural environment and traditions.

SPIRITS LIQUID AND DIVINE

The Christian spirit that is so much in evidence – and still very much alive – is not the only spirit for which Islay is famous. The distilled spirit we call single malt whisky is one of Islay's great contributions to civilisation – something the island has given back after a long history when it had to absorb so many outside influences.

Above: Dun Chroisprig and Machir Bay

There's lots to do, and lots to see. Islay is a place to which holiday-makers return again and again, often passing on their love of the island to succeeding generations. The constantly changing climate has its drawbacks, especially in winter, but most people are grateful for the constantly changing landscapes, as weather patterns reveal nuances of light and shade that cause even the locals to pause and be grateful that they live in such a beautiful place. It can be harsh and unforgiving too, but even the rain has a softness.

It's an island with a long history. The landscape is permeated with the remains of Islay's past. The standing stones and hill-forts of prehistoric times sometimes can only hint at who built them, but the dozens of Christian sites are testimony to 1,500 years of spirituality, interrupted but not destroyed by Norse occupation in the Middle Ages – eventually Islay's violent Vikings settled down and adopted the religion of the locals.

With the well-defined peninsulas of the Oa and the Rinns, and with sea-lochs nearly cutting the island in half, Islay has natural divisions dictated by its geography, and we follow these in our travels around the island. In addition, in Chapter 6 we have a day out on Jura, the next island to the north, rugged and barely populated, a stark contrast to Islay in almost every way.

At one time in its history Islay was the capital of a kingdom. Today it seems remote, on the very edge of Europe, but in the Middle Ages the MacDonald Lords of the Isles ruled their sea-kingdom from Finlaggan in Islay, at one time controlling almost all the west coast of Scotland and all the offshore islands. Gaelic culture came close to obliteration with the clearances and emigrations of the nineteenth century, but at the very end of the twentieth century there is something of a revival going on, and it is beginning to look as if the tide of decline has turned.

Stacking peat for collection at Ballinaby

In this book we try to give you enough background, enough of an appetite, to make your visit more enjoyable; but in the end, it is up to you to make the most of the opportunities you find – for example, by taking advantage of good weather and making the most of the long summer days, for in the summer months it is still light until nearly midnight, and the early mornings are a magical time.

This book does not attempt to fill in *all* the fascinating and interesting details of the island's past, but we provide enough to make you want to know more. You can find more about Islay either by reading – a further reading list is provided at the end of the book – or just by being there and exploring the island, and meeting its people. You will find either of these approaches very rewarding, although many of the books written about Islay are out of print and difficult to obtain – except through your public library. And as for exploring Islay, it's the task of a lifetime to do it thoroughly, and you will never run out of surprises.

Left: Rocks at the south end of Machir Bay

1 UNRAVELLING TOPOGRAPHY:
AN INTRODUCTION TO ISLAY

THE ISLAND OF ISLAY lies in the southern Hebrides, off the west coast of Scotland, in the former county of Argyll. Islay is a diamond-shaped jewel in the western ocean, shaped and sculpted by the last Ice Age and battered on its western side by the forces of Atlantic storms. Two long sea-lochs, Loch Gruinart on the north coast, and Loch Indaal on the south, nearly cleave the diamond in two. Sometimes the resulting shape is described rather unglamorously as a witch carrying a bag of coal on her back.

Islay has outstanding appeal for a wide spectrum of visitors. It's easy to get to, with a full range of accommodation and services and a large enough population (3,540) to allow more diversity and choice than on most Hebridean islands. With clean air and unpolluted water, and spectacular scenery, it is an ideal destination for the town-dweller seeking escape, peace and tranquillity.

Islay offers the hill-walker a splendid choice of excursions and is internationally famous for its bird life: the rare chough breeds there, and flocks of migrant geese are easily seen. Over 270 species of birds have been recorded on the island, including about 110 breeding species. The island's landscape is interesting and varied, providing a range of habitats for birds and animals, and an interesting diversity for amateur geologists or pebble-gatherers. All around are poignant reminders of Islay's historical past, from the enigmatic standing stones and cairns of antiquity to shepherds' cottages abandoned within living memory. The ruins of Dunivaig Castle and the memories preserved in the Museum of Islay Life evoke Islay's past glories, when as Queen of the Hebrides (in Gaelic, *Banrigh Innse Gall*) it was the centre of the Lords of the Isles, who ruled the whole of the Western Isles and much of the western seaboard of Scotland from their capital at Finlaggan for much of the Middle Ages.

The ruins and remnants in Islay's landscape hint at a turbulent and often bloody past. But the birdwatchers at Traigh Ghruineart see no signs of the blood spilt there in the clan battle of 1598, while

AN ISLAND'S ATTRACTION

Whatever the weather, and whatever the time of year, there is always on Islay that added attraction that comes from visiting an island – the feeling that you are cut off from the world. This isolation can be invigorating and refreshing, and apparently addictive, for many visitors return again and again, year after year. Often they have some personal connection with the island: perhaps a grandparent who left to work in the factories or shipyards of central Scotland, or a more remote ancestor who left in search of a better life in North Carolina, Texas, Canada, Australia or New Zealand.

Left: Rock formations at Machir Bay
Below: Chambered cairn at Cragabus

the picnickers at Blackrock or Machrie see no trace of the Viking longships which once were beached on these idyllic strands.

On the west side of the island, the pounding Atlantic surf attracts surfing enthusiasts to beaches where the sea-rollers surge unrelentingly, reminders of the power of nature – which is a much more immediate concern on an Atlantic island than in the tamed safety of a mainland town. Islay's weather can be overpowering, whether in the full blow of a winter storm or in the amazing shimmering sight of Loch Indaal on a hot, clear summer's day. But when the forces of nature seem invincible, and the human spirit is worn down by the battle, consolation can be found in the product of Islay's eight distilleries, in the form of a well-deserved dram of single malt whisky, whose medicinal and restorative value has been eloquently attested to by generations of connoisseurs.

The Islay ferry at Kennacraig

While most visitors come in the summer months, when the weather can range from idyllic to abysmal, an increasing number of people are coming to the island in the 'off' season. Birdwatchers come to see the winter visitors and migrants, while archaeologists revel in the opportunity to visit sites without struggling in waist-high bracken.

The sheer size and scale of Islay comes as something of a surprise to some travellers. From Portnahaven at the south end of the Rinns peninsula to Ardtalla at the end of the Kildalton road is over 37 miles (60km), while from the Mull of Oa to Bunnahabhainn in the north-east is over 31 miles (50km). There is plenty to explore, and endless nooks and crannies to be discovered and shared. Off the beaten track there are all sorts of interesting possibilities, and with a little preparation and research and a lot of local advice the rewards can be immense.

It is difficult to imagine anybody leaving Islay disappointed with their visit. From the first kindly welcome to the final glimpse of distant hills on the journey home, visitors will be captivated and entranced by what they see;

and undoubtedly they will find that the island has worked its magic on them, and that they are for ever under its spell.

Getting to Islay is straightforward enough, but requires some forward planning. Most people go by ferry from the Caledonian MacBrayne ferry terminal at Kennacraig on the Argyll mainland. There are usually two sailings every day except Sunday: the early morning one to Port Ellen and the early afternoon one to Port Askaig. On Sundays there is usually a single round trip, though there are extra sailings at the weekend in the summer months. On Wednesdays during the summer season the ferry sails to Port Askaig, then on to Colonsay and Oban, returning to Kennacraig in the evening.

Intending visitors should check their travel arrangements carefully; the confirmation of bookings for motor vehicles is *essential*. Cancelled sailings due to bad weather are unusual, even in winter, but can unavoidably occur at any time of year. Calmac's office at Kennacraig (tel 01880 730253) will be able to give up-to-date information on ferry services and to make bookings if necessary.

It is also possible to fly from Glasgow Airport to Glenegedale on Islay, halfway between Port Ellen and Bowmore. The flight time is only forty minutes, compared to over five hours by bus and ferry, so it is well patronised, despite the extra costs.

However, the ferry trip to Islay (on a good day!) is an experience not to be missed, full of interest and amazing scenery. As the boat leaves the shelter of West Loch Tarbert and the Argyll mainland, the prominent hilltop on the port side is Dun Skeig, on top of which are three successive Iron Age hill-forts, guarding the entrance to an important seaway. Half an hour later the island of Gigha comes into view, as the ferry passes its northern point. (Gigha has its own ferry, from the Kintyre village of Tayinloan.) On reach-

TO ISLAY BY YACHT

A small but increasing number of people arrive on Islay in their own yachts, or on sailing holiday charters, often en route to more exotic and remote destinations. Both of Islay's ports are well used to the yachting fraternity. However, Hebridean waters are treacherous and amateur mariners must be able to calculate tide tables. The combination of quirky weather and tricky navigation can be demanding, but provides enthusiasts with some of the best sailing in UK coastal waters.

En route to Islay

ing the open sea you can feel the constant swell of the North Atlantic, even on a 'calm' day; after a storm the trip can be quite dramatic.

Off to the north-west are the Paps of Jura – conical quartzite peaks visible over a wide arc of south-west Scotland. Their name dates from before 1600 at the very least, and possibly derives from prehistoric fertility cults on the island of Jura.

Most morning sailings head for Port Ellen, on the southern coast of Islay. As the ferry approaches Port Ellen, the white buildings of the distillery villages of Lagavulin and Ardbeg are prominent. The land stretches away to Ardmore Point to the east, while ahead of us is the Oa peninsula.

Overleaf: Port Ellen

THE ROAD TO BOWMORE

The road from Port Ellen north to Bowmore is deceptive, especially for the first-time traveller: the first mile out of the village is dead straight, with a nasty dog-leg at the end of it, and then there follows another long straight stretch of road, over eight miles in all, where the temptation is to put one's foot down – but this road, though straight, is far from level, and a few bone-shattering bumps and jolts will quickly slow the traveller down, or at least test a car's suspension to its limits! The reason for this is that the road is built for the most part on a peat bog, and is literally floating on the peat in places, causing uneven subsidence and making for a rough ride.

Gigha is now well astern, a low-lying island looking like the humps of a sea monster. On a clear day the Mull of Kintyre can be seen stretching off to the south-east, while the coastline of Antrim lies to the south-west. To the east, directly astern, the mountains of the island of Arran in the Firth of Clyde peek over the low peninsula of Kintyre. As the ferry passes the island of Texa, the scatter of houses at Port Ellen comes into view, along with the nearby distillery village of Laphroaig.

On the port side entering Port Ellen, the strangely shaped lighthouse of Carraig Fhada stands out, looking more like a war memorial or an ancient temple than a warning to navigators. You can also see the gravestones and chapel at Kilnaughton, further along that shore. In the trees at the head of the bay is Carnmore House. Nearing the pier, the large metal sheds of Port Ellen distillery and its associated maltings loom large.

The visitor arriving at Port Ellen is using Islay's 'front door'. The village is well provided with shops and hotel accommodation; there is also a garage and a Post Office, and a Community Information Office – a useful place to find out what's on, and where.

The road east from Port Ellen passes through the distillery villages of Laphroaig, Lagavulin and Ardbeg on its way to Kildalton and Ardtalla. The castle of Dunivaig at Lagavulin was a stronghold of the MacDonald Lords of the Isles. The medieval church at Kildalton is a roofless ruin now, but beside it is the ninth-century High Cross, a masterpiece of Early Christian stone-carving.

West of Port Ellen a road runs to Kintra and the Oa peninsula (the 'a' is not pronounced); at one time over four hundred people lived in this area, where now there are just a few scattered farms.

On the west side of the road from Port Ellen and Bowmore is the luxury Machrie Hotel, with a golf course and five miles of unspoiled beach

Ferry arriving at Port Askaig

on its doorstep. A little further north is Islay's airport at Glenegedale, served twice daily from Glasgow. On the east side of the road, two miles north of the airport, is Duich Moss, the cause of much controversy some years ago as distillers, farmers, naturalists, conservationists, politicians and Greenland white- fronted geese vied for superiority – and publicity – in a conflict which was perhaps more apparent than real. More recently, common sense seems to have prevailed, and everybody's interests have been protected.

The alternative port of entry to Islay is Port Askaig, on the north-east coast of the island halfway up the Sound of Islay, the sea passage between the islands of Islay and Jura. Here the tide flows like a fast-flowing river, and the ferry sails close to the Islay shore to avoid both prevailing westerly gales and the worst of the tidal currents. This is perhaps a more interesting ferry route,

The ferry from Jura to Islay, taken from Port Askaig

and frequently more sheltered. Indeed in rough weather, Port Ellen sailings are often diverted to Port Askaig, sometimes at short notice. The route passes close to the lighthouse on MacArthur's Head, perched on its cliff edge.

Just before arriving at Port Askaig the Iron Age fort of Dun Bhoraraig is visible on a coastal ridge. Dating from perhaps 200BC, it was once a broch – a tall tower of stone – but is now a mound of rubble. However, it is the only monument of its kind on Islay, is fairly easy to get to, and is well worth a visit. Quite a lot of architectural detail has survived, if you know where to look.

Just to the south of the pier at Port Askaig is Dunlossit House, unseen from the public road but with an open aspect to the stunning views up and

THE OVERLAND ROUTE

One day the Jura ferry might form one link in an alternative route to Islay known as the 'overland' route, because most of the journey would be by car, with two short ferry crossings. A specially designed rough-water ferry carrying twenty cars, proven in the stormy waters around Shetland, could ply the short crossing between Lagg in Jura and Keills at the entrance to Loch Sween on the mainland south of Tayvallich, cutting the journey time to Lochgilphead and Glasgow by almost an hour. The backers of this idea claim that the frequent service this 'overland' route could provide would greatly benefit both Islay's farmers and others with business on the mainland, and would be significantly cheaper both in travel costs and more importantly in additional expenses – at present a trip to Glasgow from Islay involves two overnight stays; even a journey to Campbeltown or Lochgilphead involves staying overnight on the mainland.

Proponents of this 'overland' route stress that the link from Port Ellen to Kennacraig would be maintained, specialising in heavy freight, though also carrying cars and passengers. Some folk in Port Ellen are anxious about a decline in tourist traffic, but it is generally agreed that the 'overland' route would benefit the people of Islay. However, the major drawback with this scheme is the tremendous costs that would be incurred in upgrading the single-track roads in both Jura and Knapdale.

down the Sound of Islay and to the mountains of Jura. Port Askaig itself has one small shop, one hotel, and not much else. The Port Askaig Inn, a warm, friendly hostelry, accepts 'well-behaved dogs' as well as the more usual assortment of guests. The pier offices are very basic, so there's not much to do while waiting for the ferry except enjoy the view.

The small car ferry to Jura sails from Port Askaig across the Sound of Islay to Feolin. The crossing takes about ten minutes. A day spent exploring Jura by car, returning to Islay in the evening, is well worthwhile. The mountains of Jura dominate the landscape at the southern end of that island. The three largest hills are Beinn an Oir (2,571ft; 784m), Beinn Shiantaidh (2,477ft; 755m), and Beinn a'Chaolais (2,407ft; 734m).

2 THE ISLAND'S CAPITAL AND CROSSROADS

BOWMORE

WHETHER ARRIVING BY SEA at Port Askaig or Port Ellen, or by air at Glenegedale, it is likely that most visitors will head for the town of Bowmore, the island's administrative capital and main shopping centre. The Tourist Information Centre in The Square is the first essential port of call. Here a good range of leaflets and brochures is available, and a very attractive tourist map of the island. This office is open from May to September (tel 0149 681 254).

The main street of Bowmore runs from the harbour to the famous 'Round Church' at the top of the hill. This is the parish church of the united parishes of Killarrow and Kilmeny, built in 1767 by Daniel Campbell, the principal Laird of Islay. It replaced the medieval parish church which was located at the head of Loch Indaal; the old site now lies in the grounds of Islay House, at Bridgend.

Above: Bowmore High Street

Right: Bowmore Distillery

The internal arrangement and furnishings of the Round Church reflect remodelling in the late nineteenth century and later. The octagonal tower and stone cupola fit well into the traditions of eighteenth-century Scottish civic architecture (as at Dysart, in Fife), and there is no reason to suppose that a foreign architect was employed, despite local belief to the contrary. A more folksy explanation of the Round Church is that it was built that way so there would be no corners for the devil to hide in. Whatever the truth, it is a very beautiful building, very striking, and something of an architectural gem. Recent restoration and redecorating of its whitewashed exterior have greatly enhanced its appearance.

Just off The Square in Bowmore is another whitewashed complex of buildings with a spiritual ambience; some would say that the quality of the spirit involved is just as intangible. The buildings of Bowmore Distillery, surmounted by the distinctive 'pagoda' roof, produce a particularly fine version of malt whisky – the 'amber nectar' – using peat for fuel and other traditional methods. A Reception Centre is well used by islanders for functions of different kinds. In summer, tours of the distillery start here, and these give a most interesting insight into the technology of whisky distilling.

As a result of first the generosity of Morrison Bowmore Distillers Ltd and the Mactaggart family, and also the monumental fund-raising efforts of the entire population of Islay, the Mactaggart Pool was opened in 1993 in a redundant distillery warehouse. Local authorities and Highlands and

SHOPPING IN BOWMORE

Bowmore's many small shops and craft outlets deserve further investigation. For outdoor types, the Islay Farmers shop on the north edge of the village will solve all practical problems. Back in The Square, the Roy emporium, known as The Celtic House, is a great place to browse for books, good quality gifts and souvenirs, knitwear and leisurewear; reproductions of the 'Great Seal of the Lords of the Isles' and of the 'Kildalton cross' are of particular interest. The proprietor, Mr Colin 'Pat' Roy, is a member of a very old and enterprising Islay family. Other aspects of the Roy empire on Islay include a bakery, a craft shop and restaurant, and holiday houses and offices.

Islands Enterprise were similarly cajoled, bullied and eventually persuaded into matching the funds raised locally. This award-winning building contains a 25m swimming pool and is a major new addition to Islay's facilities. Certainly the island's children greatly appreciate learning to swim in a heated swimming pool, rather than in the sea as previously. Small wonder that so many islanders never learned to swim at all!

The small harbour at Bowmore is an ideal destination for an evening stroll, after dinner in one of the town's excellent hotels or eating places. The sunset over Loch Indaal, with the lights of Port Charlotte and Bruichladdich twinkling on the farther shore, is a sight which reduces returning exiles to tears and has tourists reaching for their cameras. The view of the white-washed fortress of Bowmore Distillery highlighted by the evening sun, and the Round Church at the top of the hill, with the smell of peat fires – the peat reek – wafting down from the village, is an experience to preserve in the memory.

Just to the south of the distillery is Islay High School, to which scholars are bussed from all corners of the island. It was given sixth-year status in 1974; prior to that, senior pupils had to go to the mainland to complete their secondary education. The school roll numbers around 300, with the authorities always hoping that enough young adults will return to add to their qualifications so that cut-backs can be avoided. Architecturally the school mirrors the distillery, with the pagoda roof of its new extension completing its silhouette as seen from the centre of the village. There, The Square is an attractive place to sit and watch the world go by, while waiting for the public telephones or contemplating a visit to the bank, the Tourist Information Centre, or the local shops.

There is an interesting and undemanding walk along the loch to the south of the town, ideal after a meal of scallops, prawns, venison or delicious local lamb – local restaurants and hotels have been making much more of an effort in recent years to market local produce (only a few years ago this meant lasagne and chips and a local malt whisky). Details of walking excursions can be found in an excellent little booklet prepared by the Islay and Jura Marketing Group; some are listed at the end of this book, too.

Leaving Bowmore to the north on the Bridgend road, the Paps of Jura are seen straight ahead in clear weather. The main road swings around the tidal flats at the head of Loch Indaal, and this is one of the best places on the island to see the migrant geese. From mid-October to mid-April over 30,000 geese spend the winter on Islay. Thousands can be seen at the head of Loch Indaal and in the Gruinart area, to the north-west of Bridgend. During late autumn days, birdwatchers and ornithological researchers can be seen in strategically placed laybys, counting the geese through their telescopes and binoculars; some of the geese are ringed, and the three-letter code on the plastic ring is clearly visible up to half a mile away, viewed through a powerful telescope.

Left: Bowmore Round Church and (above) the interior

IAIN OG ILE

Overlooking this scene at the head of Loch Indaal is a monument to John Francis Campbell (1821–85), the folklorist and Gaelic scholar. He was a true Victorian polymath. Known throughout Gaeldom as Iain Og Ile – Young John of Islay – he was the son of Walter Frederick Campbell, the last Shawfield Laird of Islay, but found himself dispossessed of his inheritance at the age of twenty-six. After his father's death the estate was found to be bankrupt and had to be sold, leaving the young John to seek his career elsewhere. Instead of becoming the next Laird of Islay, he studied at Edinburgh University, and here he was introduced to the fields of optics and photography that were to interest him all his life. In 1851 he qualified in law, and was called to the Bar of the Inner Temple in London. It was not a choice of career which he relished. He wrote of himself that his talents lay in other areas: 'a gift of tongues, an artist's uncultivated talent, a fondness for natural science of all sorts and a very active strong body'.

In London he was looked after by his cousin, the 8th Duke of Argyll, and the combination of this patronage, his earlier scientific training, and his legal qualifications opened doors for him as the secretary of various Royal Commissions, which were a popular mid-Victorian pastime for experts with a social conscience. He served on the Royal Commission on Heating and Ventilating which looked into living conditions in both civilian and military life, and then on the Lighthouse Commission and the Coal Commission, and the multi-volume reports of all these bodies were largely John Francis Campbell's own work. These public service appointments provided him with a steady income, and the long parliamentary recesses gave him an opportunity to see the world. He travelled extensively in Scandinavia on several occasions and also visited Iceland, the Faroe Islands, and Russia. In 1874 he completed a world tour by way of North America, Japan, China, south-east Asia and India. Everywhere he went he kept copious journals, all of them profusely illustrated by his own watercolours and sketches, and thus providing a fascinating record of the lands in which he travelled, as well as frequently being of a high artistic standard in themselves.

From 1860 to 1880 he was a member of the Royal Household, carrying out various courtly duties at Windsor, in London, and occasionally at Osborne on the Isle of Wight. It is recorded that he discussed the geology of glaciation with Queen Victoria!

Not much is known about his personal life. He never married, probably more from extreme shyness coupled with financial insecurity in his twenties than from any aversion to women. He spent long periods of his later years in the south of France, and died at Cannes in 1885, probably from tuberculosis. His grave there is marked by a replica of the Kildalton cross.

Although he was a world traveller and respected public figure, it was as a collector and publisher of Gaelic folk tales that his major achievements lay. His *Popular Tales of the West Highlands* (4 vols, 1860–2; reprinted in

CAMPBELL THE SCIENTIST

In the scientific arena Campbell interested himself in the problem of recording hours of sunshine, and he is remembered as the inventor of a device which came to be known as the Campbell-Stokes sunshine recorder: it was subsequently improved by Sir George G. Stokes, a distinguished mathematician and optical physicist. He also published several papers on the subject of glaciation, drawing on his experiences around the world.

1983–4) provide an excellent window into the Gaelic world for English speakers, as well as containing cracking good stories. He adopted a scholarly approach to the study of folklore, and was familiar with parallels from other parts of the world. A large number of his informants came from Islay, many of them known personally to him from his boyhood days at Islay House. However, he recruited widely throughout the Highlands and Islands, through his network of friends. Few of his informants could read or write, and most of them understood only Gaelic. For accuracy in translation he relied heavily on contributions from Hector MacNeill, the Ballygrant schoolmaster who had been his boyhood tutor, though his own proficiency in Gaelic was considerable. He was careful to print tales exactly as they were spoken, resisting attempts from some quarters to 'correct' the Gaelic of the story-tellers: 'I know the difference between spoken and written Gaelic which no one but a native can appreciate and my book is meant to be vernacular.'

He argued vigorously against the claim by James Macpherson to have rediscovered poetry by the Gaelic epic poet Ossian, and regarded the controversy as a sterile argument which held back Gaelic scholarship. He campaigned strongly for a Chair of Celtic at Edinburgh University – a post to which some of his friends felt he was unlucky not to have been appointed.

The obelisk standing on the hill overlooking Loch Indaal was erected in his memory by An Comunn Ileach, the Islay Association. The first monument collapsed in a gale in 1911; the present monument with its striking bronze bust was the replacement. It is reached by turning up the

The John Francis Campbell Monument at Bridgend. The inscription on the monument reads in part: 'An eminent Scholar, Linguist, Scientist, & Traveller; A true Patriotic Highlander; Loved alike by Peer and Peasant' – all in all, very 'Victorian' sentiments!

CHILDHOOD AND ACHIEVEMENTS

Despite his privileged upbringing, John Francis Campbell spent his earliest childhood years in the company of the ordinary people of Islay. In the introduction to his Popular Tales he describes those early years in Islay:

> *I learned to be hardy and healthy and I learned Gaelic. I learned to swim and to take care of myself, and to talk to everybody who chose to talk to me. My kilted nurse and I were always walking about in foul weather or fair, and every man, woman or child in the place had something to say to us. Thus I made early acquaintance with a blind fiddler who could recite stories. I worked with the carpenters; I played shinty with all the boys about the farm; and so I got to know a good deal about the ways of Highlanders by growing up as a Highlander myself.*

In 1985 the centenary of Campbell's death was marked by a major exhibition at the National Library of Scotland in Edinburgh; this drew heavily on his unpublished journals and manuscripts to bring his achievements to a wider public for the first time. A leaflet prepared for the Museum of Islay Life lists his publications and identifies which of the Popular Tales came from Islay, with a list of the Islay contributors.

Mullindry road, just past Ceannloch House, with access through the second gate on the south side of the road; then a short walk leads to the monument itself. From here there is a panoramic view of the north end of Islay: Bowmore lies two miles to the south-west, the outline of its harbour, Round Church and distillery towers clearly visible. On the north is the extensive area of woodland around Bridgend; and behind that, as always, the Paps of Jura. To the west, across the tidal flats at the head of Loch Indaal, lie the Rinns of Islay, where nearly half the local population still speak Gaelic.

Gaelic language and culture is experiencing something of a revival in Scotland, with government funding for television and radio programming, and a flourishing of Gaelic drama, poetry, art and literature. In 1891 the main language of Islay was Gaelic, spoken by over 85 per cent of the population. Today, as in the rest of the Southern Isles, the language of our grandparents is in decline, although proportionately it survives better in Islay than its neighbours. According to the 1981 census, 43 per cent of today's Ilich speak Gaelic; in Kilchoman parish, in the Rinns, over 50 per cent can still speak the language. However, it is also the case that 28 per cent of the population in that parish are aged over 60.

Of course, the crude census percentages disguise the fact that the actual number of people speaking Gaelic has been reduced drastically since 1891. In that year the number of Gaelic speakers in Islay was at least 6,000, while today it is no more than 1,720 out of the total population of just over 3,500. Islay High School is committed to doing everything it can to promote the use of Gaelic: three-quarters of the pupils have at least one Gaelic-speaking parent, and all are taught the language in the first two years of secondary school; in the fourth year, half the school takes Gaelic.

A couple of miles up the back road behind the Campbell obelisk is Islay's most spectacular prehistoric monument: Dun Nosebridge. The somewhat strange name arises from an English surveyor's version of a Gaelic speaker's misunderstanding of a Norse name. 'Dun' (pronounced 'doon') is the Gaelic word for a fort; 'Nosebridge' comes either from the Norse 'Knaus-borg', the fort on the crag, or possibly from 'Hnaus-borg' – turf fort. The end result is a tautological concoction which is just confusing.

The fort itself is on top of a prominent rocky crag, slightly D-shaped, consisting of a rubble wall enclosing the summit area which measures 25 by 15m. The ridge on which it sits is aligned north-east to south-west, with steep cliffs on the south-east flank. On the remaining sides two ramparts, ditches and subsidiary enclosures provide added protection. Dun Nosebridge dominates the surrounding countryside, and although it is almost certainly originally an Iron Age fort (perhaps 850–500BC), it is very likely that it was an important centre during the Norse occupation of Islay (AD800–1150). However, this remains to be proved. It is common enough for Norse (and Gaelic) place-names to be given to prehistoric monuments, so it is probably a mistake to attach too much importance to its strange name, whatever it was originally.

BRIDGEND

FOLLOWING THE MAIN ROAD past John Francis Campbell's obelisk, the big white house on the edge of the Bridgend woods is the Islay Estates office where the factor or estate manager lives. A little further on is the village of Bridgend consisting of a hotel, a general store, a couple of other shops, a bowling green and not much else. On the outskirts of the village is where Islay's farmers assemble their livestock for auctions, and across the road from the stock pens is one entrance to Islay House, the biggest 'Big House' on the island, and recently sold off by the estate. The village of Kilarrow once stood on the shore here, but the Campbell laird who built Islay House decided it would improve his view if these houses were removed, so the population was shifted to Bowmore in the eighteenth century. The old medieval parish church and its burial ground are still there, however, with many sculptured medieval grave-slabs scattered amongst the later graves – unfortunately mostly in very worn condition.

In order to make it easy for the laird and his family to enjoy the grounds of Islay House without having to cross the public road, a massive bridge, resembling an aqueduct, was built across the main road on the edge of the village; however, it has recently been demolished to improve the corner for juggernauts.

Here the main road divides, with the A846 road through Bridgend continuing under the now non-existent bridge and heading for Port Askaig, while at the T-junction just past the general store (which sells Sunday papers – on Sunday!) the A847 turns south, heading for the Rinns peninsula.

Above: Dun Nosebridge and (overleaf) East from Dun Nosebridge. The mountain peak is Glas Bheinn

GAELIC CULTURE

Gaelic culture is promoted in several ways. Islay hosts what is known as 'Feis Ile', featuring music, song and dance from the 'Celtic Fringe' with workshops in Gaelic language and music. The annual whisky-tasting night, featuring all the Islay malts, is an added attraction. There is also an annual drama festival in Gaelic, and Gaelic choirs always draw good attendances for their concerts. During the summer season, the 'ceilidh' (pronounced kay-li) is a feature of island life – not the spontaneous, informal social gathering where songs and stories would be exchanged, but the more organised modern equivalent to be found in the evenings in the larger hotels.

3 Distilleries and
Early Christians

Lagavulin Distillery

Port Ellen is Islay's main ferry terminal; most heavy freight arrives and departs from here, and this is where the ferry company Caledonian MacBrayne has its main island office. It is a somewhat scattered village, arranged round a bay, with the older houses nearer the harbour and ferry pier and newer council houses on the farther side.

Travelling the single track road eastwards from Port Ellen is a pilgrimage which every visitor to Islay must make without fail. There are three distillery villages just to the east of Port Ellen: Laphroaig, Lagavulin and Ardbeg. Each produces excellent single malt whisky; each is distinctive; and each has its advocates and detractors. It can be a lot of fun making up your own mind!

UNIQUE FLAVOUR

The smoky flavour imparted from the peat fuel used in drying the barley from which whisky is made is characteristic of Islay malts, though whether a peat from one bog gives a different result as compared with a peat from any other bog is a matter of continuing debate. Laphroaig had such a distinctive flavour that it was actually imported legally into the United States during Prohibition as a 'medicinal spirit'! It has sometimes been criticised for being too medicinal, but its fame and continuing popularity speak for themselves.

As the second-largest employer in Islay (after agriculture), the whisky industry is vital to the island's economy. An industry-wide recession in the 1980s caused closures and cut-backs at distilleries throughout Scotland, and Islay was no exception. The industry has always been vulnerable to market forces, and this is not the first time that it has gone through a difficult period. The 1920s and 1930s saw the truncation of the Scottish whisky industry, while during the years of World War II production was severely controlled and restricted. In Islay today distillery managers are cautiously optimistic that they will survive the present bad patch, and that through improving managerial and technical efficiency they will overcome recent problems.

The mood of confidence underlying recent caution is based on the quality of the product. Islay malt whisky is distinctive, some would say superb, and they would be right! The method of production is basically unchanged over the last two hundred years, though some distilleries have modernised some aspects of their operations. They are of course loath to do anything which might jeopardise the integrity of their product, for successful marketing is helped immeasurably by emphasising the traditional aspects. On the other hand those distilleries which *have* modernised their plant and equipment can still succeed through good marketing – and the quality of their product.

The 'pagoda' roofs which are a traditional feature of whisky distilleries provide ventilation to the malt kilns. As we have already noted, the architect of the extension at Bowmore High School, which is just along the road from Bowmore Distillery, successfully incorporated this feature into his design.

Another important tradition is that whisky should be aged or matured in former sherry casks made of oak. Whisky must mature for at least three years before it can legally be sold, though most people involved in the industry in either production or consumption would argue that it should be left for at least five years. After ten years it becomes even more smooth and palatable, and these improvements are naturally reflected in the price.

Laphroaig and Bowmore still use traditional malting floors on which the barley is regularly turned by hand and raked with a special tool over a seven-day period to control germination. However, only about 50 per cent of their malting requirements are produced in this way, and until recently the rest was imported in bulk from commercial malt producers in Scotland and Ireland. But the economics of importing malt at a transport cost of over £30 a ton compared badly with the haulage cost of around £3 a ton from the Port Ellen Maltings, which was operating at far below capacity after the closures and short-time working at distilleries owned by Scottish Malt Distillers: realising this, all the distilleries in Islay have formed a consortium to rationalise the situation, a move which naturally benefits all concerned.

There is an unbroken tradition of legal distilling stretching back to the eighteenth century in Islay. The earliest record is of Bowmore Distillery in 1779, but it is very likely that distilling started in Bowmore before that, soon after the foundation of the village in 1768. Lagavulin was a very early distillery, though the records of the early years are sparse. Of course illicit small-scale distilling existed long before that, and may just possibly have continued for long after – some say up to the present day! The Museum of Islay Life displays a small pot still which came from the hills somewhere behind McArthur's Head; the donor would not reveal the exact location.

The possibilities of raising revenue for the state from the consumption of whisky were realised by Oliver Cromwell, who imposed an excise tax of twopence a gallon. However it was not until the eighteenth century that closer control of production was sought, and it was not until 1817, when a modest tax on output was substituted for the previous repressive tax on capacity, that illicit stills started to disappear, though they continued in a small way.

ISLAY'S DISTILLERIES

Reference books suggest that up to twenty-three distilleries may have existed on Islay, some of them very small and transitory. At present there are seven working distilleries on the island: we have already mentioned the three east of Port Ellen (Laphroaig, Lagavulin and Ardbeg), there are two further distilleries on the shores of Loch Indaal, at Bruichladdich and Bowmore, and two more on the coast north of Port Askaig, at Caol Ila and Bunnahabhainn.

Above: The tun room at Bowmore distillery and (left) the still house

Everybody connected with the industry views Budget Day with apprehension, for the Chancellor of the Exchequer is only too well aware of the revenue possibilities of excise tax on whisky. When the industry is struggling to build up its exports, extra taxes do not help the situation, while if the tax remains stable it is a matter of great relief, if not celebration. There has always been a certain amount of resentment that Scotland's national drink should be regarded as a luxury drink by the Treasury; does not its very name derive from the Gaelic '*uisge-beatha*', the 'water of life'?

Bowmore Distillery gives the impression of being one of the best-run, and also one of the most innovative distilleries in Scotland – for example 'waste' heat is used to good effect at the adjoining swimming pool in a renovated warehouse, and the Reception Centre built in 1974 is well used as a venue for meetings and functions. Undoubtedly the best way to understand the process of whisky distilling is to visit a distillery. It's best to telephone in advance if you would like a tour as some of the smaller concerns do not really have the resources to cope with tourists, while some of the older ones are in buildings not really suitable for visitors. Bowmore Distillery is best equipped to show people around, offering regular tours from Easter to September with full-time guides – and a well-stocked distillery shop.

Lagavulin has the most interesting setting, with an important and picturesque castle right on its doorstep. Dunivaig Castle (spelled Dunyveg on the OS map) was an important stronghold of the medieval Lords of the Isles, and is easy of access. The crumbling stone keep dates from the seventeenth century, and should be avoided; for historians the really 'interesting' feature of the site is the earlier medieval castle with its now ruinous 'curtain' wall. It is there because of the excellent anchorage of Lagavulin Bay, where the Lords of the Isles could keep their naval force safe from the elements and out of sight of potential enemies.

Bowmore Distillery shop

Right: Port Ellen Maltings

Far right: Dunivaig Castle

KILDALTON

CONTINUE along the coastal road, looking out for herons, seals and sea birds, and so head for Kildalton church, a late medieval roofless ruin beside which is Islay's most famous treasure, the ninth-century High Cross of Kildalton, hewn from a single slab of local stone and a masterpiece of stone-carving.

Although a little weathered, the Kildalton cross is unbroken and well enough preserved to enable us to recognise quite a lot of the detail of the carvings. It is carved from a single slab of local grey-green epidiorite containing granules of felspar, and its slightly asymmetrical appearance is due to the sculptor following the grain of the stone. The west face is richly decorated with raised, carved bosses, one in the form of a 'bird's nest' containing three small 'eggs' representing the Trinity. The east face is covered with richly carved figures. The scene in the left arm of the cross shows Cain murdering Abel with a jawbone as he kneels, offering his sacrifice to God. The right arm of the cross shows the sacrifice of Isaac by Abraham on a square altar. The upper arm has two angels, David killing a lion, and two birds pecking at a bunch of grapes. At the top of the shaft a scene showing the Virgin and Child is flanked by two angels.

The theme of this wheel-cross is sacrifice, and it is easy to imagine a priest using it as a kind of visual aid in explaining the message of the Bible to parishioners. The style of the Kildalton cross is closely related to three of the major crosses at Iona – St Oran's, St John's and St Martin's, and must surely have been carved on Islay by a sculptor from the Iona workshops. Like the Iona crosses, it probably dates from around AD800. Islay came under the sphere of influence of the 'Columban' church, and there is evidence of its monastic influences on Islay at Kilchoman, Nereabolls, Kilarrow, and Kildalton, and on the offshore islands of Texa, Orsay and Nave. So there was undoubtedly a monastic foundation at Kildalton in the Early Christian period, although no surface traces remain. The ruined medieval church was probably built in the late twelfth or early thirteenth century, under the patronage of the Lords of the Isles. Some idea of what they might have looked like can be obtained from the stone effigy grave-slab of a man in armour inside the medieval church. The walls and both gables survive almost to their full height, with some of the dressed stones coming from the out crops of Old Red Sandstone near Machrihanish in Kintyre.

A visit to Islay without seeing the Kildalton cross is unthinkable, but those readers unfortunate enough not to see it, for whatever reason, might like to know that concrete and plaster casts may be viewed in the Royal Museum of Scotland, Queen Street, Edinburgh (formerly the National Museum of Antiquities of Scotland) and in Glasgow Art Gallery and Museum (Kelvingrove). Historically and artistically, this cross is of outstanding national importance.

HISTORY IN THE NAME

The name 'Kildalton' (Cill Daltan meaning 'the church of the foster-child or disciple') probably refers to St John the Evangelist, the 'beloved disciple'. The dedication in medieval sources was to St John, and its modern successor in Port Ellen is St John's. Included in the name there may also be the idea that Kildalton was the monastic 'foster-child' of the monastery at Iona, but scholars dismiss this as 'attractive but unconvincing'. Alternatively there may just have been an individual named Daltan associated with the early monastery, though there is no trace of him anywhere else in the Celtic world.

Grave-slab in Kildalton church

Left: Kildalton Cross

RITUAL TORTURE

When the foundations of the Kildalton cross were being repaired and reconstructed in 1882, some human remains were found which it was thought at the time showed evidence that the victim had been 'spreadeagled' – as the historian W.D. Lamont delicately puts it, 'a singularly unpleasant sport to which the Vikings were addicted'. This form of ritual torture involved the 'blood eagle': the victim was pinned to the ground, face down, and his heart and lungs removed, from the back, and held aloft. As this gruesome death was reserved for important or valorous victims considered worthy of honour, it has been suggested that the remains underneath the Kildalton cross may have been of the abbot of the monastery. Vikings started looting Hebridean monasteries from AD801 onwards; within twenty years the ruthlessness of their attacks forced the church authorities to retreat to Ireland with their treasures, abandoning their parishioners to their fate. The Viking raids were followed by centuries of Norse occupation.

Across a farm track from the church and graveyard at Kildalton is another cross, smaller and carved in a different style. It is late medieval (1350–1500), and apparently unfinished.

When visiting Kildalton it is worth allowing time to continue along the main road another mile and a half to Claggain Bay. Geologists will have a field day there, and anybody who appreciates pretty stones will find that the variety of beach pebbles makes it a fascinating place to spend a summer's afternoon – though it can be a bit exposed and windswept in winter. The northern and southern arms of this bay are guarded by Iron Age vitrified forts of similar design.

It is thought that originally the walls of these forts were built with a timber framework to provide extra stability and strength, which if it caught fire left vitrified, glassy material in the wall core. The causes and origins of the vitrified forts and duns of Scotland have been the subject of controversy since the phenomenon was first recognised in the nineteenth century. For vitrification to occur, the stone rubble of the wall core has to have been heated to a very high temperature, sufficient actually to melt the stone and cause it to fuse into a distinctive glassy mass. Because the end result is an incredibly strong mass of rock, it was thought initially that this must be a construction technique, designed to improve the defences of a site. However, a combination of evidence from archaeological excavations and from experimental archaeology in which timber-laced ramparts were built and fired, has led most of today's researchers to conclude that vitrified walls are the result either of the carelessness of the inhabitants or the aggression of attackers. The presence of silica in the rock of which the walls are built is essential for true vitrification to occur; in other cases the stones of the wall would simply redden and crack if the wall were fired.

Claggain Bay – pebbles on the beach

Right: Kildalton church and crosses

THE OA

The American Monument on the Mull of Oa

TO THE WEST of Port Ellen a single-track road wends its way across the middle of the Oa (the 'a' is not pronounced) peninsula, through what is now an almost deserted wilderness but was once home to over four hundred people. After a mile or two this road divides, one spur leading to Kilnaughton and Carraig Fhada lighthouse to the south, the other to Kintra Farm to the north. Both of these roads are well worth exploring. Beyond Carraig Fhada, which in itself is an amazing intrusion into the traditional vernacular architecture, there is a short walk to a sandy beach whose grains interestingly produce a 'singing' effect when scuffed with the soles of your shoes. At Kintra, there are endless miles of sandy beach and sand dunes, and a highly diversified farm which also boasts an excellent restaurant.

The first farm on the Oa road is Cragabus, a Norse name and so presumably a Norse farmstead during their occupation of Islay, AD800–1150. But we know there were farmers there long before that, because

Previous page: Kilnaughton Bay and Carraig Fhada lighthouse

across the road from the modern farm are the remains of a Neolithic chambered cairn, one of only six in Islay, the burial place of the first farmers on the island dating from perhaps 3500–3000BC. The cairn of stones which once covered this monument is gone, quarried for dyke-building, but the burial chamber is still there, well defined by large stone slabs. When it was examined in 1901 it yielded up no bones, which would have been long decayed, but only a few sherds of pottery, seventeen flint flakes, a flint core, and a white quartz pebble. The finds are now in an Edinburgh museum. Although there is not all that much to see, it is worth stopping for a look, because with a little imagination you can begin to realise that this was once an imposing monument in which the local community must have invested thousands of hours of work.

The road over the Oa ends at Upper Killeyan Farm, where a car park is provided. From there you can walk for a mile to the Mull of Oa, which is marked by the American Monument commemorating the 266 Americans drowned when HMS *Tuscania* was torpedoed seven miles off the coast on 5 February 1918. The view is superb; to the south-west is the coastline of Antrim.

What happened to the local population? Most of them ended up in Canada, assisted in their emigration by their well-meaning but ultimately uncomprehending laird. This was not a 'Highland Clearance' in the sense that people were burned out of their houses amid scenes of brutality and suffering, as happened in Sutherland and elsewhere, but the effect on the native population was no less traumatic. A Gaelic song describes the journey in 1862 of the emigrant ship *Venus* from Port Ellen to Canada, from the point of view of one of the few who stayed behind. The Laird John Ramsay of Kildalton visited them in 1870 where they had settled on the shores of Lake Huron, Lake Simcoe and Georgian Bay.

Chapel by Kilnaughton Bay and Carraig Fhada lighthouse

While the Oa peninsula was almost emptied of its human population (who were replaced by sheep and shepherds), other parts of Islay also suffered dramatic depopulation. While the population of the island today is around 4,000 it is thought that it may have reached a peak at around 10,000 in the middle of the nineteenth century – far more than the island could support – and many thousands left for what they hoped would be a better life in Canada, the United States, Australia and New Zealand. Their descendants return every year, seeking their roots. Of course, not everybody who left Islay ended up in a foreign colony; more thousands migrated to central Scotland to work in the shipyards and factories of the Clyde.

Also, many people left long before the emigrant rush of the 1840s and 1850s. Some had gone to New York a century earlier in 1738, while in 1739 settlers from Islay, Jura and Kintyre established themselves in the Cape Fear area of North Carolina. This is all fairly well documented, compared to other parts of Scotland, and locally produced lists from cemetery inscriptions and censuses assist in reconstructing family trees.

The way in which the problem of overpopulation was worked out in Islay by the Morrison and Ramsay lairds illustrates very well the fact that Islay was, and still is, not exactly typical of Hebridean communities. Islay was sufficiently large and self-contained to produce its own variant of a solution. In particular, problems of land tenure were solved, one way or another, in a fairly amicable if patriarchal way, so that when the Crofting Act of 1886 was implemented in an attempt to curb the worst excesses and to guarantee security of tenure in the Highlands and Islands, this did not have any significant effect on Islay. In general, Islay was never a crofting community in the sense of smallholdings for crofter-fishermen coupled with common grazing rights. Due to the policies of the Campbells, Morrisons and Ramsays, Islay farms were largely single-tenanted by 1880.

It is perhaps worth mentioning in passing that there is nothing 'traditional' about the crofting system. The traditional system in the Highlands and Islands was communal, with lands held in common by a township, paying its rents as a community. Moreover, the term 'croft' refers to a holding of land, not to the dwelling-house which may or may not be situated on the land. The old township has now died out completely in Scotland, though crofting townships in some islands recreate something of the old sense of community and cooperation which existed at one time. An important feature of the old system was the spring migration to upland grazing, when the whole community would move to upland pastures, leaving behind only those too old to travel to look after the township until the end of the summer and the harvesting. Field evidence of this system of transhumance can be seen in moorland areas, often on south-facing slopes or in sheltered positions beside streams, in the form of small beehive-shaped turf dwellings known as 'shielings', These were normally only big enough for one or two people to shelter for the night, though larger, quite elaborate ones are also found. Shielings found in the upper reaches of glens now remote and deserted are often a clue to the existence of an abandoned township in the flatter, cultivated ground further down the valley.

Many visitors to Islay will pass the Auchindrain Museum, situated on the mainland of Argyll between Inveraray and Furnace, on the road down Loch Fyne. Here, a township in the old style somehow survived until the 1960s, and a fine open-air museum and interpretative centre helps to recreate a way of life once universal in the Highlands and Islands. An hour or two spent there will help visitors prepare for their island holiday.

Right: The view north from the Mull of Oa

4 THE LORDS OF THE ISLES – AND MORE DISTILLERIES

THE VILLAGE OF BRIDGEND lies at the head of Loch Indaal and here the main road divides, with one branch turning north and the other heading for the Rinns peninsula. The main road north leads to Port Askaig, Islay's other ferry terminal, with secondary roads turning off at Ballygrant and just before Port Askaig for Lossit and the distillery villages of Caol Ila and Bunnahabhainn.

After leaving Bridgend the north road passes the entrance to Islay House and its Home Farm, then one of the island's rural primary schools at Newton. The first road on the right leads to a woollen mill, still partly in operation, with an associated shop. It is well worth a visit for the insight it gives into an important part of Islay's industrial history.

BALLYGRANT

BALLYGRANT is a small village with a hotel and shop; the houses are rather spread out along the main road, with firstly a small group of council houses and then the older houses of the original village situated at a crossroads. Here a side road to the south-east leads to Lossit Farm, from where access is possible to Dun Bhoraraig, Islay's only Iron Age broch. Enough remains of this once imposing stone tower to make one marvel at the engineering technology employed over two thousand years ago. Dun Bhoraraig stands on a prominent hill, 619ft (189m) above the Sound of Islay, with commanding views over the surrounding land and sea. It is courteous and desirable to enquire at Lossit Farm before visiting this site.

Brochs were towers of drystone construction, standing up to 13m (48ft) high and achieving their height because of their ingenious hollow-wall construction. The best surviving example is at Mousa, in Shetland, while other relatively well-preserved brochs can be seen at Carloway, in Lewis, and near Glenelg, on the mainland of Scotland opposite the Isle of Skye. There are hundreds of more dilapidated examples concentrated in Caithness, the Northern Isles, Skye, and the Hebrides. The exact location of their origin within this area is a matter of lively debate amongst archaeologists, but there is general agreement as to their likely date, which is from about 100BC to AD200.

ISLAY'S DIVERSITY

The woodland around Bridgend and Islay House may come as something of a surprise. It is a mistake to think of all Hebridean islands as windswept and treeless, because given shelter and good land management the mild climate often allows localised pockets of deciduous woodland to flourish. It is frequently said that the most appealing thing about Islay is the diversity of its landscape – but then, of all the Hebridean islands it is the only one big and fertile enough to accommodate such a wide range of landscapes and habitats; other islands may contain some of the varied elements involved, but only Islay has them all. The same could be said of the range of archaeological and historical remains, from stone circles to castles.

Left: From near Dun Bhoraraig looking south-east over the Sound of Islay

When Thomas Pennant visited Dun Bhoraraig in 1771 the walls survived to a height of 14ft (4.3m) and were 12ft (3.6m) thick, with galleries inside the wall visible all round. There has been considerable collapse and stone-robbing since then, but enough of the site remains to identify many of the typical features of a broch: the design of the entrance passage, a guard-chamber, a 'scarcement ledge' (supporting a floor), and the thick, drystone, 'hollow' wall. It is well worth a visit today, despite the depredations of time and the local dyke-builders who quarried it for building stone.

The name is a hybrid place-name, incorporating the Gaelic 'dun' meaning 'fort', and the Norse 'borg-ar + vik' – 'the bay of the fort'. The Vikings were a sea-people and often identified landmarks, anchorages, harbours and topographical features visible from the sea. The Norse settlers who followed in the wake of the sea-raiders added their own distinctive settlement names; there are dozens of examples of Norse farm-names on Islay, and presumably the remains of Norse homesteads lie underneath more recent buildings at these locations. The names which give the clearest evidence of Norse settlement are those containing the Old Norse element *bolstadr*, a farm. Over the centuries the Norse word has been absorbed and abbreviated, appearing in today's place-names in such diverse forms as -bister, -bost, or -bus, or sometimes as -boll or -pol. There are about forty -bus endings on Islay; farms like Coillabus, Cornabus, Cragabus, Risabus and Persabus, or Nereabolls, Stanepoll and Torrabol are very likely to have been founded by Norse settlers in the tenth century AD. The place-name evidence shows us that hundreds if not thousands of Norse settlers lived on Islay. But Dun Bhoraraig was already in ruins when the first Norse people arrived in Islay.

Back at Ballygrant, another fork of the Lossit road leads past the old farm of Knocklearach to Storakaig and the valley of the Laggan River which runs past the fort of Dun Nosebridge and into the sea near Bowmore.

FINLAGGAN

BACK ON THE MAIN ROAD and a mile past Ballygrant is the turn-off for Finlaggan, the administrative capital of the medieval MacDonald Lords of the Isles. Take the Mulreesh farm road, and after half a mile, turn left for Finlaggan. After a few hundred yards a farm track leads to a car park and a renovated cottage used as an interpretative centre by the Finlaggan Trust.

As you park your car beside Finlaggan farmhouse, you will see Finlaggan Loch stretching off to the south-west. At the north end of the loch are two small islands, and it is here that the Lords of the Isles had their island headquarters. Access is by a small boat, provided by the Finlaggan Trust, to the larger of the islands, Eilean Mor ('the big island'). On it are the upstanding remains of two buildings, a chapel and a hall, and the turf-covered remains of over thirty other structures of various periods.

Right: Dun Bhoraraig and the hills to the south

The ruined chapel and grave-slabs at Finlaggan

MEDIEVAL GRAVE-SLABS

Similar carved grave-slabs are found in other graveyards on Islay, though nowhere so well preserved as at Finlaggan. They are also found up and down the length of the west coast of Scotland, from Lewis in the north to the Mull of Kintyre in the south, and are now known to have been carved in workshops at Iona, Oronsay, Kilmartin and Saddell (Kintyre), under the patronage of the Lords of the Isles.

The chapel is the better preserved building, though roofless and partially collapsed. It lies on the highest point of the island, and on the flat ground beside it is a graveyard – look here for the square stone base on which there once stood a carved stone cross; the shaft of this cross, which would have contained information about who erected it and whom it was commemorating, has yet to be found. However, another beautifully carved cross-head was found during archaeological excavations and is displayed in the Finlaggan Cottage.

On slightly sloping ground just beneath it are a number of elaborately carved, late medieval grave-slabs dating from 1350 to 1500. These are decorated with swords, galleys, plant-scroll and other motifs; the most spectacular stone is an effigy of a man in armour dating from around 1500 – the Latin inscription, part of which is now broken, translates as 'Here lies Donald, son of Patrick, son of Celestinus'.

To the south of Eilean Mor and at one time connected to it by a stone causeway, is Eilean na Comhairle ('the Council Isle'): where the Lords of the Isles and their Council of fourteen members deliberated at a stone table, issuing edicts, instructions and rulings affecting their territories, and administering justice. Traces of a well-built stone castle with thick, encircling walls have been found on this small islet.

At the height of their powers, in the first half of the fifteenth century, the Lords of the Isles – at that time also Earls of Ross – ruled all the islands off the west coast of Scotland and a good part of the coastal mainland from Cape Wrath to the Mull of Kintyre. Theirs was a sea-kingdom, depending on naval power for defence and using well established coastal sea routes to keep control of their far-flung domains.

Old records refer to gatherings of thousands of people at Finlaggan on important occasions such as the inauguration ceremony of the Lords of the Isles. Legally these western territories belonged to Norway until the Treaty of Perth (1266), but in 1156 a local warlord, Somerled, whose father was a Gael but whose mother was Norse, defeated the local ruler of the Hebrides in a sea

Grave-slabs at Finlaggan

battle and assumed control for himself. The man he defeated was Olaf, King of the Isle of Man, who functioned as the Norse 'Governor' of these increasingly isolated territories. Somerled married Olaf's daughter, and headed an invasion of mainland Scotland in 1164, leading a large force of galleys and fighting men up the Clyde to Renfrew, where he was murdered by treachery before he could bring the Scots to battle.

Somerled's grandson, Donald, is the Lord of the Isles from whom all the MacDonalds in the world get their name. The last MacDonald Lord of the Isles was John, and he came to pose a major threat to the mainland Scottish kingdom by making a treaty with Edward IV of England in 1462. When this came to light in 1475 the lordship was threatened with obliteration by an extremely displeased Scottish king, and John was summoned to Edinburgh where he had literally to crawl on his hands and knees and ask for forgiveness. He was allowed a second chance, but had to give up Kintyre and Ross. In 1493 things blew up again, possibly as a result of an attempt by John to regain the earldom of Ross; or perhaps the king, now James IV, simply lost patience with his renegade western subjects. In any event, all the lands of the lordship were forfeited by the Scottish Parliament, reverted to the Crown, and were redistributed. James IV undertook a series of campaigns in the west, determined to put an end to a challenge which had been a thorn in the side of Scottish kings for two hundred years.

Archaeological dig at Finlaggan

There are interesting sites to visit on the shores of Finlaggan Loch. Halfway down the eastern shore are the remains of lead workings, while overlooking the western side is a deserted village, abandoned in the nineteenth century during the emigrations. On the way back to the main road, look for the remains of lead mines and workings; these mines, which also produced silver in small amounts, date back to the Middle Ages and were not finally abandoned until 1880.

Bunnahabhainn

KEILLS AND MORE DISTILLERIES

CONTINUE ALONG THE MAIN ROAD towards Port Askaig and you will come to the village of Keills, built beside the ruined medieval church which gives the village its name. The older houses were built in 1829 to accommodate weavers from Glasgow, and a lint mill provided to convert flax into linen. These houses are still there, with more recent council houses in the gaps between the original holdings.

A mile before Port Askaig is the turn-off for Bunnahabhainn, pronounced 'Bu-na-ha-venn'. One of Scotland's most remote whisky distilleries lies three miles up a winding single-track road, with passing places to escape from the enormous, articulated distillery lorries. The new generation of vehicular ferries has revolutionised transport on Islay: at one time almost all distillery traffic came by sea, and each distillery had its own pier.

There are some stunning views from the Bunnahabhainn road. The scenery to the east is dominated by the Paps of Jura, often modestly hidden in swirling mist but frequently exposed to the full light of day, their cones of quartzite gleaming in the sun. By walking a few yards off the road, the full length of the Sound of Islay can be seen. To the north, Colonsay is visible behind the Rhuvaal lighthouse, and the mountains of Mull can be seen over the raised beaches of Jura.

Previous page: The chapel at Keills, with Jura beyond

Just half a mile before Port Askaig is the road to the Caol Ila distillery, lying on the Sound of Islay from which it takes its name. The Gaelic 'caol' is often rendered as 'kyle' in place-names, which is more or less how it is pronounced. 'Ila', which means 'of Islay', is pronounced 'eela'. This distillery has been completely modernised in recent years, a welcome investment in the long-term future of the industry.

Looking over Bunnahabhainn to the Paps of Jura

PORT ASKAIG

PORT ASKAIG is just a ferry terminal, shop and hotel. It is also the base for the Islay lifeboat, and the RLNI flag flies proudly from the flagpole in front of the hotel; since the lifeboat station was established in 1934 the Islay lifeboat has saved over three hundred lives. In 1979 a new 50ft Thames-class self-righting lifeboat was commissioned, the *Helmut Schroder of Dunlossit*, named by his son Bruno Schroder of Dunlossit House, its generous sponsor and benefactor. It has twin spade rudders for maximum manoeuvrability, a maximum speed of 18 knots, and a range of 205 nautical miles at full speed. It normally carries a crew of six.

Its design was put to the test later that year on the night of 17–18 November when it capsized in mountainous seas while attending the Danish coaster *Lone Dania* in distress off the north-west of Islay. This was the first occasion on which the self-righting capabilities of the new class of lifeboat had been tested in actual storm conditions, so it was immensely gratifying to all concerned to find out that the design actually worked. The conditions were appalling: winds gusting to force 11/12 – hurricane force – with thirty-foot waves occasionally rising to twice that height. The Barra lifeboat also capsized when responding to the same incident, but also managed to right itself; its self-righting design was of earlier date and made use of inflatable bags. The

BEWARE SHOOTING!

During the shooting season visitors would be well advised to check with the offices of the various estates regarding access to the hills. Farmers, local hotels, or the Tourist Information Centre in Bowmore may also be able to advise as to which areas may be safely visited.

Honorary Secretary of the Islay branch of the RNLI at the time was Frank Spears of the Port Askaig Hotel; it was his responsibility to launch the lifeboat, and that night he bore an extra personal interest because his son was in the crew. These brave men – all volunteers – who put their lives on the line to save mariners (*and* the annual crop of idiotic yachtsmen) get tremendous support from the local community. Contributing to their funds is one way in which visitors can show their appreciation to an island community which needs all the support it can get.

North of the Bridgend–Port Askaig road there is a line of hill farms and then wilderness with only occasional tracks. Alternate heather moor and peat bog makes for difficult and tiring walking, and distances can be very deceptive. Youth and long legs are definitely advantages in this terrain. From the road end at Bunnahabhainn it is possible to walk across open moorland to the north coast of Islay, where the main attractions are caves, raised beaches, seabird colonies, and fantastic scenery. The view from the top of Sgarbh Breac (1,192ft; 364m) is superb.

The south-east corner of Islay is also a wilderness, except for the narrow coastal strip from Port Ellen to Ardtalla. The view from the summit of Islay's highest hill, Beinn Bheigeir (1,609ft; 491m), is a panorama of moorland and hill-lochs on one side, and of a seascape dominated by the Paps of Jura on the other. In the distance, to the east, can be seen the lands of Knapdale and Kintyre with the peaks of Arran beyond, while to the south-west the coastline of Ireland is usually visible. The most interesting ascent is from the south-east, up the Claggain River.

The Port Askaig lifeboat

5 MEDIEVAL SPLENDOUR IN A GAELIC PENINSULA

Raised beach by Loch Indaal, to the west of Black Rock

THE AREA KNOWN AS THE RINNS OF ISLAY has its own separate identity – indeed in pre-glacial times, that is before 10,000BC, it was a separate island. The road from Bridgend runs along the shore of Loch Indaal, passing one of the finest aspects of a raised beach in the country at the head of the loch. There are side roads leading to Ballinaby, Smaul and Kilchoman, but the main road continues along Loch Indaal, reaching the twin distillery villages of Bruichladdich and Port Charlotte. At the end of the peninsula are two more villages: Portnahaven and Port Wemyss.

The north end of the Rinns – the area around Loch Gorm, between Kilchoman, Ballinaby and Sanaigmore – and the road to Ardnave up the west shore of Loch Gruinart are among the most scenic and historically interesting parts of Islay.

KILNAVE

THE ROAD TO KILNAVE passes the RSPB centre at Aoradh Farm, from where information on birdwatching and tours of different bird habitats are available. The late medieval chapel at Kilnave, with its Early Christian free-standing cross, is set in a magnificent scenic location. On a reasonably clear day the low-lying islands of Colonsay and Oronsay are visible, eight miles off the north coast of Islay, while the Paps of Jura peep over the hills on the east side of Loch Gruinart.

This is a good area for wildlife. Between October and May the fields around Kilnave are grazing grounds for geese and other migrating birds, while all sorts of waders enjoy the tidal flats on the shores of Loch Gruinart. Seals, or 'selches' (selkies) as they were called in the old Scots tongue, were noticed here by one of the earliest visitors to write about Islay, Donald Monro, Dean of the Isles: writing in 1549, he commented that 'upon the bankes [of Loch Gruinart] upon the sea lyes infinit selccheis, whilkis are slain with doges lernt to the same effect'; though he does not mention what kinds of dogs were thus used. In 1776 it was said that it was not worth the expense of a net to try to catch salmon at the entrance to Loch Gruinart, as seals there were killing so many fish.

The weather-worn stone cross in Kilnave churchyard, recently conserved, stands 2.63m (8.5ft) high. Although much of the decoration has flaked off and bits of the arms are missing, enough survives to show that this was a very fine piece of sculpture in the Irish tradition, probably carved by a sculptor trained in an Irish school. A date of AD750 has been suggested for the Kilnave cross.

The roofless chapel at Kilnave (Cill Naoimh 'the church or burial ground of the saint') dates from the twelfth century. The round-headed windows were arched by thin slabs of stone rubble, and the interior of the building was covered originally by a thick coat of wall plaster.

MACDONALDS V MACLEANS

ON A HOT AUGUST DAY in 1598 Kilnave was the scene of a bloody skirmish between the Macleans of Mull and the MacDonalds of Islay, the culmination of decades of skirmishing and squabbling between the two clans over their rights of ownership of certain lands in the Rinns of Islay. The story contains more turns and twists of fate than ever entered the mind of the most imaginative soap-opera script writer.

Right: The cross and medieval chapel at Kilnave

Briefly, the MacDonalds of Islay, the Lords of the Isles, had lost all their territories in Islay and elsewhere in 1493: as a result of years of misbehaviour and treason, all had reverted to the Scottish Crown. It took twenty years to make an inventory of all the forfeited estates, which were then granted under charters to loyal and reliable tenants, mostly various branches of Clan Campbell. In Islay, the lands of the Rinns were granted to the Macleans of Duart in Mull, while other lands in Islay were given to a branch of Clan Donald, the MacIans of Ardnamurchan, who were considered reliable because their chief was married to a Campbell. But in 1567 Angus MacDonald succeeded to the chieftaincy of the Islay branch of Clan Donald, and in 1578 his rival Lachlan Maclean of Duart, came of age; these two larger-than-life characters, and their followers and relations, were to keep this area of the Western Isles in turmoil and upheaval for the best part of fifty years.

In 1579 Angus MacDonald married Lachlan Maclean's sister, at the insistence of the government, and it was hoped that this imposed relationship would put an end to the quarrel between the two clans. But on a visit to Duart Castle, Angus was taken prisoner and held there until he agreed to sign away his claim to the Rinns of Islay; on his release he had to leave his son James and his brother Ranald as hostages. Soon after, Lachlan arrived in Islay, with young James, to assert his claim to the Rinns. But Angus MacDonald neatly turned the tables, and at a banquet in their honour Lachlan and eighty-six of his followers were arrested. Back in Mull, one of Lachlan's kinsmen, Alan Maclean, saw his chance to assume the Maclean chieftancy. He let it be thought that Ranald MacDonald, Angus's brother, had been put to death in revenge, hoping that the MacDonalds would take out their anger on the captive Macleans. His scheme very nearly worked, as the eighty-seven Macleans on Islay were put to death at the rate of two a day until only Lachlan was left alive. It wasn't until the very last minute that news of Alan Maclean's deception leaked out – and Lachlan's execution had been delayed only because Angus MacDonald had an accident on the way to witness his brother-in-law's end.

In a portent of some significance, James VI appointed various important members of Clan Campbell to act as mediators. In 1587 Angus MacDonald released Lachlan Maclean in a deal which involved the transfer of eight Maclean hostages to Islay. But the totally incorrigible Lachlan immediately raided Islay, after which Angus raided Mull and Tiree in retaliation. However, while mustering his forces for another attack on Mull, Angus was surprised by a Maclean attack at his rendezvous at the south end of the island of Kerrera, near Oban; among the prisoners were MacDonald of Sleat (in Skye), Macleod of Lewis, and 'McFee of Collowsay' (Colonsay).

Again the King tried to impose a settlement, but Angus MacDonald refused to hand back his eight hostages, and was therefore outlawed. Lachlan Maclean agreed terms with the King but he too soon renewed the feud. In 1588 MacIan of Ardnamurchan, an ally of the MacDonalds of Islay, was to marry Lachlan Maclean's mother. However, during the wedding

Left: Looking through the east window of Kilnave chapel

festivities Lachlan ordered all the MacDonalds present to be massacred – only the bridegroom was spared. Then he raided the islands of Rum, Eigg, Canna and Muck, apparently with the help of some Spanish mercenaries whose galleon was anchored at Tobermory on its way home from the debacle of the Spanish Armada. This expedition reportedly exterminated the population of the four islands. Angus MacDonald invaded Mull with a band of English mercenaries, but after some skirmishing an agreement was reached, and Angus exchanged his eight hostages for MacIan and some other prisoners.

The King had had enough. In 1589 the Macleans and MacDonalds were summoned to Edinburgh, arrested despite assurances of pardon for past offences, and promises extracted. Angus MacDonald's son, James, was to remain in Edinburgh, where he became a favourite at court and was later knighted. In the islands the peace held only until 1592, when a revolt of Scottish nobles diverted attention and tempted the feuding parties to resume hostilities. But Parliament summoned them for treason in 1592, and sentenced them to forfeiture in 1594. Angus MacDonald, by now an old man, schemed with his kinsmen in Antrim and even with the English, but in the end gave in and agreed to behave himself, after his son Sir James MacDonald was sent from Edinburgh to reason with him.

However, the exasperated King had leased the Rinns of Islay to Lachlan Maclean, which he was legally entitled to do since the MacDonald lands had been forfeited and so reverted to the Crown. In 1597 old Angus went to Edinburgh and made his peace with the King. He was to give up Kintyre and the Rinns of Islay, give security for payment of the arrears of Crown rents, and give up Dunivaig Castle to the King's nominee, while Sir James, his son, would remain at Court in Edinburgh for further security. Part of the settlement reads:

> His majestie sall have full libertie with the said Angus and his sonis consent, to dispone upoun the landis of Ilay noch sett to Makclane, and also upoun the haill ilis of Jura and Colanza and upoun the said fourtie merkland adjacent to Kilkarrane, as his Majestie sall think gud for planting of burrow townis with civile people, religioun, and traffique of merchandice thairupoun.

In other words, civilisation was about to be imposed. But the failure of the MacDonalds to retain control of their ancestral lands was to mean further upheavals in southern Argyll.

Ironically, Sir James MacDonald was to be the main cause of this upheaval. Early in 1598 his father Angus had still not handed over his Kintyre estates, and Sir James, the King's favourite, decided to bring him to book. He cornered his father in his house at Askomel, at Kilkerran in Kintyre – now part of the Royal Burgh of Campbeltown, one of the 'burrow townis' envisaged by James VI. It was founded in 1609 and subsequently settled by reliable Protestant merchants and farmers from Ayrshire and Renfrewshire.

Sir James was determined to bring his father in, and old Angus walked unwittingly into a trap. Sir James was staying at the farm of Smerby, two miles north of Kilkerran (Campbeltown), with his old friend John McKay, when his father arrived at Askomel from Islay. Hearing that his son was nearby, Angus walked over to Smerby to visit, spending over two hours in his son's company. No doubt suitably lubricated against the cold of a January night, it was after midnight when Angus left Smerby. By the time he got home to his house at Askomel, his wife was fast asleep in bed.

They and their household were rudely awakened 'about the dawning of the day' by a commotion outside. According to a contemporary witness there were 300 men around the house, armed 'with hagbuittis, pistolletis, axes, bowes, targeis, two handit swordis and uther invasive wapines'. The door of Askomel House was securely locked and bolted, but Sir James pounded on the door, demanding his father's surrender. Angus politely declined, whereupon his son and his followers set fire to four different parts of the house.

Sir James's mother Finwall Maclean (Lachlan's sister) and the rest of the household escaped unharmed. The old man refused to yield, but eventually he was forced to make a run for it, or he would have been burned alive. As it was, he was burned 'on three or four parts of his body and on his shoulder', and his shirt was badly singed front and back. Sir James had 'laid trees afore the house door purposely' to cause Angus to 'fall on his outcoming'. Angus rushed out of the house, tripped on the 'trees', and was duly captured. He was put into iron chains and imprisoned first at Smerby, then in Saddell Castle for two nights, and finally safely delivered to the royal castle at Dumbarton.

Unfortunately for Sir James, the authorities did not share his enthusiasm, or approve of his methods. Public opinion was outraged, old Angus was pardoned, and he was released on promises of good behaviour, having allegedly suffered enough. But five years later he was to turn the tables on his son: he captured him in Islay and handed him over to Campbell of Auchinbreck, who took him to the Earl of Argyll, who delivered him to the Privy Council in Perth; where, for his excess of zeal at Askomel, he was charged with wilful fire-raising and treason.

After the outrage at Askomel, Sir James had fled to Islay. Meanwhile Lachlan Maclean had decided to take advantage of the MacDonalds' infighting to extend his hold on Islay. In August 1598 the two sides fought each other at what has become known as the Battle of Traigh Ghruineart (Gaelic for 'the shore of Gruinart').

The story of what happened has been preserved in oral tradition in Islay, handed down by word of mouth over the generations. As the two sides were preparing for battle, a dark-skinned hunch-backed dwarf of black, hairy appearance came to Lachlan Maclean and offered his services as an archer. His father was a Shaw from Jura and his mother, it was said, was a

DEFORMITY IN FOLKLORE

The magical motif in the story is maintained by introducing the Dubh Sith, who was most probably not the son of a fairy woman but a MacDuffie with a physical deformity. Supernatural intervention, especially by the Devil, was often introduced in Highland folklore to explain mental or physical deformity. The name MacDuffie derives from the Gaelic 'Mac Dubh Sithe'; 'Shaw' in the Traigh Ghruineart story is just another version of the 'Sithe' element in that name.

fairy woman. He was called in Gaelic 'Dubh Sith'; to the people of Islay his name meant 'black fairy'. He had to twist his ugly head to look up at Lachlan, who reputedly stood over seven feet tall. Maclean treated him with contempt and declined his offer of help – the Macleans outnumbered the MacDonalds and he was confident of victory.

So the dwarf sought out Sir James MacDonald and offered his services to him, and this time he was gratefully received. The Dubh Sith said that if the MacDonalds looked after the rest, he would take care of Lachlan Maclean. He climbed up a into a rowan tree beside a well, and waited.

The battle was fought on a hot, August day, and during a lull in the hostilities Lachlan Maclean made his way to the well for a cooling drink. As he removed his helmet and knelt to drink, the Dubh Sith took his chance and shot a bolt from his crossbow straight into the back of Maclean's neck at such an angle that the tip came out at his eye. With their leader dead, the Macleans lost heart, and although Sir James MacDonald was himself wounded, the MacDonald forces took the upper hand and routed their opposition. The Macleans sought sanctuary at the church at Kilnave, but in their thirst for vengeance the MacDonalds set fire to the thatched roof. All the Macleans inside were killed except for one man, a MacMhuirich (Currie) who ran into Loch Gruinart and saved himself by submerging himself in the water and breathing through a reed. The MacDonalds thought he had drowned and left; later the exhausted man found his way ashore and was given shelter. His descendants still live in Islay, in Bowmore.

What are we to make of this tale? When clan historians put the story together, they needed some reason for Lachlan's defeat, and this they found in the idea that he had failed to heed the advice of a wise woman – always a dangerous thing to do. He had consulted her before leaving Mull and had been told not to land on Islay on a Thursday, to stay away from Loch Gruinart, and not to drink from the well known as Tobar Niall Neonaich ('the well of Strange Neil'). Lachlan ignored these warnings: having planned to arrive on a Wednesday he was in fact delayed for one day by a storm; he fought on the shore of Loch Gruinart; and he took a fatal drink at the proscribed well.

The Edinburgh authorities took a dim view of all these events. In 1603 the Scottish king became the ruler of the United Kingdom, known to English historians as James I; as a major European monarch it was not good for his image for stories of queer happenings and primitive warfare to be spread around the capitals of Europe. So when Sir James MacDonald was handed in to the authorities by his old father, he could expect to be dealt with severely.

At his trial in 1609 Sir James MacDonald was condemned to be executed as a traitor, and all his possessions were forfeited to the Crown. But the sentence of death was never carried out. Perhaps it was true that in 1598 Sir James had had a personal commission from the King to bring his father in, and that in return for keeping silence on this point his life was spared.

In 1614 old Angus MacDonald died, possibly at Rothesay, and was buried, it is said, at Saddell. His younger son, Angus, was tried and condemned for high treason and executed at Edinburgh on 8 July 1615, for his part in an abortive uprising to restore the Lordship of the Isles. Sir James escaped from Edinburgh Castle in 1615 and briefly captured some of his lands on Islay, but then was forced to flee to Spain. In 1620 he was pardoned by the King, but forbidden to return to Scotland. He made his home in London with a state pension of 1,000 gold marks a year, and died there in 1626, the year after his erstwhile royal patron.

KILCHOMAN

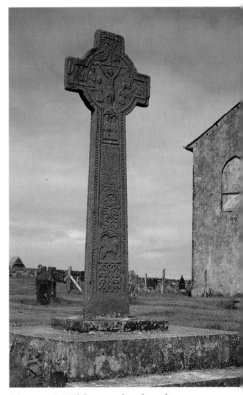

The cross in Kilchoman churchyard

ANGUS MACDONALD'S old enemy Lachlan Maclean is said to have been buried in the Rinns, at Kilchoman, after the battle in 1598. Of all the medieval sites in Islay, Kilchoman is perhaps the most rewarding to visit, although nothing at all remains of the medieval church building – or of the earlier chapel which would have been here in the sixth century. There were several Irish saints named Commán, one of them connected with Iona, and perhaps it was he who founded the church at Kilchoman in Islay. About thirty medieval grave-slabs, including some fairly small fragments, can be seen in the churchyard. Other fragments are in the Museum of Islay Life in Port Charlotte and in the Royal Museum of Scotland in Edinburgh. The most spectacular stone, however, is still at Kilchoman: a free-standing cross in its original socket-stone, situated at the south-east angle of the churchyard; it stands 2.7m (almost 8.5ft) high and is elaborately carved on both sides. It is a fine example of its kind. It is important to remember that the cross at Kilchoman is of a much later period than the crosses at Ardnave and Kildalton, which date from the eighth century AD; the Kilchoman cross was a product of the Iona school of carving, and was probably made just before 1400. It is very similar in many ways to the cross at Campbeltown in Kintyre which can be dated very precisely from its inscription to around 1380, and it is interesting to note that the Campbeltown cross has links with Kilchoman: it was erected in honour of Ivor MacEachern by his son Andrew MacEachern who was the pastor at Kilchoman from 1376 to 1382.

In one fortunate respect the Kilchoman cross is different from its counterpart in Kintyre: it is intact and unmutilated by the zealous image-smashers of the Reformation. However, the numerous fragments of cross-heads and cross-shafts which have been found in Islay show that this area was not immune from this particular manifestation of vandalism. Indeed, while crosses of the same period at Inverary and Campbeltown have had the offending images carefully chipped away leaving the rest of the carving intact, the Islay reformers seem to have favoured the more direct approach. But at Kilchoman, the figure of Christ, surrounded by saints and angels and with Mary on his right, has survived intact. Under the crucifixion

scene are two figures holding books, probably representing Tomas Beaton who commissioned the cross, and his father Patrick.

These individuals are inferred from the inscription in Lombardic capitals which, translated from Latin, reads: 'This is the cross [erected] by Thomas, son of Patrick, doctor, for the souls of his father, mother and wife, and of all the faithful departed, and of the said . . .' The very end of the inscription is worn and indecipherable. The Beaton family were well known as physicians in the West Highlands, being practically a medical dynasty, and as members of the family are known to have held land at nearby Ballinaby and elsewhere in Kilchoman parish at that time it seems reasonable to guess that they are commemorated on this cross.

On the reverse of the Kilchoman cross, facing the sea, is an amazingly intricate abstract design, with a number of patterns interlocking in a very complicated way, There is even what is thought to be a deliberate 'mistake' a slight imperfection in the way the design is worked out – this was a deliberate feature of some medieval art thought to be otherwise too presumptuous.

World War I graves at Kilchoman

Kilchoman is outstanding on a sunny day. The cliffs behind the churchyard are frequented by choughs which come to roost at dusk and which can often be seen in the area, swooping and calling in their distinctive way. There is a fine walk, too, from the churchyard towards the cemetery to the south, the cemetery itself being maintained by the Commonwealth War Graves Commission; for the most part it commemorates the captain and crew of HMS *Otranto*, lost off Islay on 6 October 1918. There are seventy graves, forty-three of them not identified. It is also possible to walk further along the shore towards Dun Chroisprig, one of the best preserved of Islay's Iron Age duns, rejoining the road system at Kilchiaran. However, it is not possible to drive a car from Kilchoman to Kilchiaran.

North of Kilchoman is Loch Gorm, with one of Sir James MacDonald's castles on a little island, and on the coast just north of Loch Gorm is Saligo Bay. Here, all fenced in, there is an aerial and buildings housing telecommunications equipment, reputedly to do with naval communications. All around lie the remains of a radio station operated during World War II, and judging from the disposition of the concrete blocks which would have anchored cables supporting radio masts, and from the remains of accommodation blocks and bunkers, this was a major wartime communications centre, presumably controlling the movements of shipping and naval forces in the North Atlantic. With its uninterrupted outlook, Islay is an obvious place to site such equipment.

Left: Detail of the cross in Kilchoman churchyard

Overleaf: Saligo Bay

CIRCLES AND
STANDING STONES

OVERLOOKING THE NORTH SHORE of Loch Gorm is the farm of
Ballinaby, one of the oldest tenancies on the island. The place-name recalls
the time when these lands were held by an abbot, since the accent is on the
third syllable. Behind the farm – but please don't visit without asking first –
is the tallest standing stone on Islay, a slim, Bronze Age monolith standing
4.9m (over 16 ft) high. There are other stones, now fallen, in a line up the

Looking towards Loch Gorm from the east

slope to the north-east, and another stone to the east. The Ballinaby stone is incredibly thin compared to its height, which emphasises its rather dramatic situation. There is plenty of scope for speculation about the meaning and purpose of these stones, but it is well understood that they were erected up and down the Atlantic coast of Scotland from Orkney right down through the Hebrides and Ireland and down the western mainland of Britain through Cornwall to Brittany, from about 2000BC to 1200BC. The great centre at Stonehenge, in Wiltshire, belongs to the same culture.

Much of the current interest and research in these strange stones was stimulated by the work of one man, Professor Alexander Thom. Sandy Thom died in 1985 at the age of ninety-three, having launched himself into

what became, in effect, a second career after he had retired from his post of Professor of Engineering Science at the Oxford University in 1961. For fifty years in all he tried to unravel the mystery of standing stones, and his sons, and eventually his grandchildren, were pressed into service, transporting theodolite and measuring equipment to some of Britain's most remote places. One result of the Thom family's labours had been an avalanche of learned articles and several books. The standing stone at Ballinaby features prominently in Thom's books – indeed, he calls it 'one of the most convincing single stone observing sites in Britain'. According to Thom, this stone was set up to record moonset halfway between the equinoxes (21 March and 21 September) and the solstices (midwinter and midsummer), and to identify the minor perturbation of the moon's orbit, which acts as a warning that eclipses may take place.

The standing stones and stone circles of the British Isles never fail to excite our imagination, and here, in the Rinns of Islay, there are fine examples of both types of monument. At Cultoon, further south on the peninsula on the back road from Port Charlotte through Kilchiaran to Portnahaven, there can be seen the remains of a stone circle, excavated in the 1970s by a team from the University of Glasgow.

The Cultoon stone circle is situated on the west side of the road from Portnahaven to Kilchiaran, and is easily accessible. There are three upright stones and twelve stones lying prone around the perimeter of an ellipse measuring 40.7 by 35.1m (133 by 115ft), or expressed in Thom's Megalithic Yards, 50 x 40. A remarkable feature of the site is that all the prone stones were lying on the old Bronze Age ground surface, now covered over by a growth of peat several feet deep.

Strangely the circle, or ellipse, was never completed. Holes were dug to take the stones, which had been brought to the site probably from the nearby shore, but most of these for some reason were never erected, the sockets were allowed to silt up, and the site was abandoned. In one case a stone had been put into its socket and then pulled out again, leading the Glasgow *Daily Record* to feature the story under the headline 'Bronze Age Vandals on Islay'. Concrete posts now mark the position of the stone sockets.

A careful search during the excavations failed to find any trace of the stakes which might have been placed in the ground at the 'nodes' of the ellipse. The excavation was conducted in truly appalling weather conditions; ironically the summer of 1976, the year after they were completed, was a real scorcher, underlining the unpredictability of our climate.

It was not always so. In the Bronze Age the weather was more settled, warmer, and more predictable than it is now, and in this context, outdoor ceremonial sites and astronomical observatories make more sense. In fact most standing stones appear to date from 1800 – 1200BC, when observing conditions were ideal. After about 1200BC there was a sudden and dramatic deterioration in the prevailing climate which led to changes in vegetation and farming practice, in due time creating the conditions which produced

PROFESSOR THOM'S CLAIMS

Professor Thom's claims about standing stones and stone circles can be divided into two main areas: firstly, that a standard unit of length (the Megalithic Yard) was used in laying out stone circles and ellipses on a geometrical framework; and secondly, that standing stones were erected primarily to track the complicated orbits of the sun and the moon, establishing an exact calendar and making eclipse predictions possible.

Left: Standing stone at Ballinaby

the peat bogs; these spread over what had been agricultural land and created the wilderness which today's conservationists so enjoy.

In many parts of Islay today it is therefore true to say that the landscape has been completely transformed since 1200bc. Traces of the underlying Bronze Age landscape can be seen at An Sithean (pronounced 'Shian') – 'the fairy knowe' – near Carnduncan, on either side of the road from Ballinaby to Loch Gruinart (B8017). Here can be seen eight hut-circles, field-banks, and clearance cairns. In the 1980s evidence was recovered from excavations of the field-banks to confirm the Bronze Age date of the field system, in two phases.

Half a mile east of the sites at An Sithean is a similar complex of sites at Glacan Daraich – 'the little dell of the oak' – and individual hut-circles and enclosures have been recorded at over thirty other locations on Islay: more no doubt remain to be discovered. Three Bronze Age houses in the sand-dunes near Ardnave were excavated between 1976 and 1980; a hearth and some pottery vessels from one of them are preserved in the Museum of Islay Life.

The kinds of monument known to archaeologists as hut-circles often survive only as heather-covered banks in upland moorland. However the finely preserved examples on Islay at An Sithean and Glacan Daraich show the stone-faced walls which served as the foundations of roundhouses; they would have been roofed by a conical framework covered with heather or reed thatching. The entrances normally face south. Of course, not all hut-circles are necessarily as old as these – the same basic roundhouse was used right through the Iron Age and well into the early Middle Ages in Argyll – but in the absence of excavation it is always notoriously difficult to date these structures.

BRUICHLADDICH

AFTER EXPLORING KILCHOMAN and the area around Loch Gorm, you have to return to Loch Indaal to continue your exploration of the Rinns of Islay. There is a fine view as you come down to the sea; turn right at the main road, and after just over a mile you arrive in the distillery village of Bruichladdich. The local malt whisky is particularly smooth and mild. However, it is very much a matter of personal preference with whisky – some people like the more robust malts, others find these too 'medicinal'. Whatever your taste, there is a well-stocked shop in the village.

On the hill above the village is the farm of Conisby, one of many farms in Islay with a Norse place-name revealing widespread settlement by Scandinavian people who came to Islay in their thousands for three hundred years after AD800. This particular farm has royal associations: 'kon-r', a 'king' or nobleman, and 'bolstadr', a farm.

It is two more miles to the next village, Port Charlotte, and exactly halfway between the two villages, in the middle of nowhere, is a church – a monument to Presbyterian thrift and confidence from a time when everybody was expected to attend every week.

Right: Looking across Loch Indaal from north of Bruichladdich. Bowmore lies on the right

TREASURE TROVE

With so much coastal erosion, and with so many sites in ever-changing sand-dunes, there is always the chance of a casual visitor finding objects of interest on historic sites on Islay. If at all possible, it is always better to leave things as they are, and seek advice from museum staff, who are used to dealing with such matters. If you do pick something up, you are under a legal obligation to hand it in to the authorities. In Scotland, any object found in the ground may be declared Treasure Trove and claimed for the Crown. Generous compensation can be paid for objects of value thus claimed, and it is always in the finder's interest to report finds as soon as possible. One should never attempt to clean objects: to do so will almost inevitably detract from their value, and very likely destroy evidence.

PORT CHARLOTTE

PORT CHARLOTTE is also a distillery village although its Lochindaal Distillery closed in 1929. It is a pretty, whitewashed village but spoilt by the large number of 'unlit houses', that is, holiday homes. The street signs are in Gaelic, reflecting the fact that the Rinns is still a stronghold of Gaelic speakers. It is extremely picturesque, with a pretty little harbour scattered about with lobster pots and fishing equipment, and wonderful views across the loch to Bowmore, or down Loch Indaal to the Oa peninsula.

This little village is home to two enterprising organisations doing their utmost to promote and present aspects of Islay to both locals and visitors. The Islay Field Centre is sited in a former distillery warehouse, and houses a youth hostel and natural history research centre, with good technical facilities, an excellent little library, and interesting exhibits interpreting the geology and natural history of Islay. Across the road is the Museum of Islay Life, in a converted church. It provides the broadest possible interpretation of human settlement on Islay, from Neolithic pottery to Edwardian bath chairs. There is an excellent reference library, available for consultation by

The Museum of Islay Life at Port Charlotte

arrangement, and an excellent archive of papers, records, maps and genealogical information. There is also a very fine collection of postcards, black and white photographs, and colour slides, covering everything from early West Highland steam-ships to last year's local festivals.

The museum was founded in 1977, and in 1980 won first prize in the Museum of the Year award for Scotland, followed by a 'special prize' in 1985 – richly deserved honours. The staff are well-organised and well-informed. Many objects from archaeological sites in Islay are displayed here. A small bookshop sells local pamphlets and guidebooks, many produced by the museum itself.

Across the road from the museum is the Port Charlotte Creamery: here, 'Dunlop'-style Islay cheese is manufactured, mostly for export, and butter for the local market. For many years the creamery was located in the old Lochindaal Distillery warehouses, but in 1981 new premises were opened. Visitors can have a tour of the creamery, though the company does appreciate advance warning of large parties. There is a small shop on the premises, where 40lb pieces of cheese will be cut to any size required; the small 1lb 'rounds' are also very popular as gifts. The creamery takes most of the island's milk production, and produces over 300 tons of cheese annually, when in full operation.

A HAVEN FOR TOURISTS

The combined tea-room and craft shop on the shore in Port Charlotte is a welcome haven for tourists on a wet day, while in fine weather the outdoor picnic-style tables and safe beach also attract visitors. The shop is well stocked with books and souvenirs, the home cooking is excellent (especially the soups), and the home-made ice-cream is superb!

KILCHIARAN

A SIDE-ROAD cuts inland at Port Charlotte, crossing the peninsula of the Rinns to Kilchiaran: here you will see the fine, late medieval chapel which has been partially restored, the walls stabilised and the altar rebuilt; several late medieval grave-slabs can be seen. The dedication is to Ciaran, an Irish contemporary of Columba in the sixth century AD, who seems to have operated mainly in Kintyre. There is no trace of the Early Christian church which would have been hereabouts; the medieval chapel dates from perhaps the fourteenth century, and despite its size was not a parish church, but a dependency of Kilchoman. A medieval font stands on a modern base inside the chapel. The medieval grave-slabs have been gathered together inside the chapel, displaying the usual combination of swords, intertwined carving and ecclesiastics.

Architecturally Kilchiaran Farm is interesting: look for the circular horse mill. And look at the futuristic buildings above Kilchiaran which contain VHF equipment for communicating with shipping – and probably a good deal more besides! The geology in this area is also worthy of note: on the beach at Kilchiaran you can see where the local Kilchiaran slates meet the much earlier Lewisian gneiss, and there are flint pebbles to be found among the millions of other stones in the shingle. Slates were quarried locally but were coarse and heavy compared to slates from, for example, Ballachulish or Easdale, and because of their weight are not considered suitable for modern houses.

The chapel at Kilchiaran

You are quite likely to see choughs in this area, as they breed on the cliffs nearby, as at Kilchoman. The chough (*Pyrrhocorax pyrrhocorax*) is a member of the crow family, distinguished by its red beak and legs, its spectacular manoeuvrability in flight and its strange call. It is rare on the Scottish mainland where it was blasted into oblivion by gamekeepers, but it still breeds on the cliffs of the Mull of Oa and on the Rinns. The species is staging a slow but steady recovery; after facing total extinction it is now beginning to spread throughout Islay and the neighbouring islands, and may soon reoccupy its former breeding sites on the Mull of Kintyre. It is probably the easiest of the rarer birds for the amateur birdwatcher to spot if patient. Choughs can be spotted almost anywhere on Islay but here at Kilchiaran, and also at Kilchoman, a sighting is assured, especially in the evening.

The back road to Kilchiaran continues on down the western side of the peninsula to Portnahaven, passing the Cultoon stone circle described above. Approaching Portnahaven there are stunning views over to the mountains of Northern Ireland.

Left: Grave-slabs and font in Kilchiaran chapel

Overleaf: Kilchiaran Bay

Portnahaven

PORTNAHAVEN AND PORT WEMYSS

RIGHT AT THE SOUTHERN END of the Rinns peninsula are the twin villages of Portnahaven and Port Wemyss. These are not pretty seaside villages but small struggling communities of lobster fishermen and farmworkers, with a few Bowmore commuters – though fewer of these than at Port Charlotte and Bruichladdich. There is no distillery at Portnahaven, so the main road has not been improved, and is still a twisty single-track obstacle course, with passing places.

As you drive carefully down the shores of Loch Indaal between Bridgend and Portnahaven it is quite likely that you will see seals basking on some of the offshore rocks and skerries. Two species of seal can be seen almost anywhere around the coasts of Islay, the common seal and the grey or Atlantic seal. The common seal is widespread and numerous, and breeds in several places around Islay's coasts. It prefers sheltered, inshore waters, and groups can often be seen sitting on offshore rocks and islets. The world population is in excess of three million. The grey seal, by contrast is one of the world's rarest seals, with a total world population of around 50,000; over half of these breeding around the coasts of Scotland, the largest Scottish

LEWISIAN GNEISS

In front of the hotel at Portnahaven there are striking expanses of Lewisian gneiss, polished by the sea – look out for small pebbles of this rock to take home and impress your friends with. It is the oldest rock in Europe, and half the age of the earth itself

Passing Places

Passing places are a widespread feature of life in the Highlands and Islands. It is not always appreciated by visiting tourists that they are intended not only to deal with oncoming traffic, but also to facilitate overtaking. It is courteous and customary to wave a cheery 'thank-you' to the driver who pulls over to allow you through. Slow-moving tourist traffic, whose priorities are different from those locals who are trying to earn a living, will be unpopular if they don't follow local custom. Also, do bear in mind as you are dawdling along a single-track road that the car behind you flashing its lights and honking its horn may very well be the local doctor on the way to a medical emergency. Fortunately visiting caravans are still uncommon on Islay.

colony being on North Rona, with a population of 7,500. A colony of several hundred breeds on the skerries south of Oronsay called Eilean nan Ron – 'Seal Island' – and they are seen regularly around Islay's shores.

Around the coasts of Islay these two species share the same habitat, but can be distinguished by their appearance and behaviour. The common seal has a much shorter face than the grey seal, and when disturbed it almost seems to turn up its nose as it looks at you; this is unlike the grey seal which has a distinctly 'Roman-nosed' appearance.

It is possible to arrange to cross from Portnahaven or Port Wemyss to the island of Orsay, where a visit to the medieval chapel and the lighthouse (built 1824–5) will provide more than adequate compensation for the time and expense involved.

Orsay from Port Wemyss

Near Portnahaven there is an experimental wave-energy research station, perhaps a prototype for a form of alternative energy which is abundantly available up and down the west coast. Of course a commercial electricity generating station would be very much larger than this discreetly

sited prototype, and an enormously intrusive feature in such a remote place. The other abundant energy source, the wind, had not so far been harnessed commercially on Islay, although it seems inevitable that it will not be long before a wind-farm is established somewhere. The whole peninsula of the Rinns is now managed in partnership between local farmers and landowners and Scottish Natural Heritage, so we can be sure that environmental and conservation considerations will be an important part of whatever decisions are taken in the future.

The villages on the Rinns, as elsewhere on Islay, owe their existence to the Campbell of Shawfield lairds who came to the island in 1726 and transformed both the island's economy and its landscape. The first Campbell laird was Daniel Campbell of Shawfield, born in Skipness but taking his title from his estates on the outskirts of Glasgow. He was a wealthy merchant, but in the forefront of the agricultural revolution which swept Scotland in the eighteenth century. He commissioned surveyors to make accurate surveys of all his farms, and introduced the flax industry to Islay. According to his grandson he also introduced a:

> Spirit of Industry into the Island of Isla, as the most proper means to Divert from, and if possible, to Eradicate the Idel-Loving and Clanish Spirit that prevailed, particularly he attended to the Raising of Flax, Built Flax Milns, Provided Flax Dressers, Hecklers, and Spinning Wheels, he encouraged Weavers, Gave Premiums to Importers of Flax Seed, and Dealers in Yarn, and to accelerate a Change to Industry, he gave his Tennants Leases for 31 years, a Term unknown to their Predecessors.

When Daniel Campbell died in 1753 he was succeeded by his grandson, known as Daniel Campbell the Younger to distinguish him from 'Great Daniel'. The new laird organised a regular ferry service to the mainland, established schools and developed the fishing and linen industries; there were also plans to develop lead, silver and copper mining. It was during his time that one of the earliest tourists came to visit Islay, and met him and described the living conditions of ordinary people; Thomas Pennant, a Welsh traveller and topographer, visited Islay in the 1770s during his tour of the Hebrides, and it is interesting to read his account of the predicament of most of Islay's inhabitants, whose situation the Shawfield lairds were trying to 'improve'. Pennant saw them as:

> . . . a set of people worn down with poverty; their habitations scenes of misery, made of loose stones; without chimnies, without doors, excepting the faggot opposed to the wind at one or other of the appertures, permitting the smoke to escape through the other, in order to prevent the pains of suffocation. The furniture perfectly corresponds: a pothook hangs from the middle of the roof, with a pot

Left: Spinning wool at Tormisdale Croft, the Rinns

pendant over a grateless fire, filled with fare that may rather be called a permission to exist, than a support of vigorous life: the inmates, as may be expected, lean, withered, dusky and smoke-dried.

Pennant describes Islay as a subsistence economy permanently on the verge of famine and starvation. Overpopulation and crop failures produced bad health and epidemics, as well as 'dropsies and cancers'. The verbal picture he paints is not a pretty one, despite his admiration for the landscape and scenery: it is a picture of a desperately impoverished society on the fringes of Europe, riddled by bad health and superstition. This was the situation that the Shawfields were trying to ameliorate.

Daniel Campbell the Younger died in 1777 at the early age of forty, having been the laird for twenty-four years. He was succeeded by his brother Walter Campbell who lived until 1816, and was thus in charge for thirty-nine years. Walter continued the policies set out by his predecessors, but the main problem he faced was one which was to become an increasing drain on his resources: overpopulation. It appears, for example , that the population rose from an estimated 5,344 in 1755 to a count of 8,364 in the first official census in 1801: an increase of 57 per cent in forty years.

Walter Campbell died in 1816 aged seventy-five and was succeeded by his grandson, Walter Frederick Campbell. Young Walter ruled until his bankruptcy in 1848, and it was under his régime that the island landscape we know took shape: farmland interspersed with small villages.

Bowmore had been founded in 1768 and Portnahaven in 1788, but the twenty years from Walter Frederick Campbell's succession saw a proliferation of small villages in Islay. In 1821 Port Ellen was started, named after the laird's first wife Eleanor. Port Charlotte followed in 1828, named after the laird's mother, then the village of Keills in 1829, built adjacent to the old medieval church which gave this settlement its name. Port Wemyss was started in 1833 – Eleanor, who died in 1832, was a daughter of the 8th Earl of Wemyss.

The population continued to increase, reaching a maximum of 15,000 in 1831; that it has fallen back to today's population of only 4,000 indicates the number of people who have left Islay in the last 150 years. Figures from the 1981 census show that about three-quarters of the population live in villages, leaving about 1,000 scattered elsewhere. The island's population appears to have stabilised at around 3,500, and is unlikely to decline further in the immediate future.

The following list gives figures for Islay villages. The figures for Bowmore and Port Ellen come from the 1981 census, with Argyll and Bute District Council giving estimates for the other settlements:

Bowmore	969
Port Ellen	1020
Port Charlotte	270

Bruichladdich	150
Ballygrant	150
Keills – Port Askaig – Caol Ila – Bunnahabhainn	270
Laphroaig – Lagavulin – Ardbeg	140
Portnahaven – Port Wemyss	130

Finally, a word about the spelling of the name of this western peninsula of Islay: is it the Rhinns or the Rinns of Islay? Older books and older maps usually have 'Rhinns', although the oldest maps of Islay, published in the seventeenth century, omit the 'h'. More recently, the official Ordnance Survey maps have revised their own nineteenth-century mistake – for the 'h' is no older than that – and opted for the Rinns of Islay; also, incidentally, for Rum rather than Rhum as the Hebridean island south of Skye. The Rinns gets its name from the Gaelic 'Roin', which means a part, or portion. As this peninsula was one of the original three portions into which Islay was divided when first settled by Gaelic-speaking settlers soon after AD300, it seems an appropriate enough term. It is interesting that there is another Rinns in Scotland, the Rinns of Galloway, also referring to a peninsula, also settled by the original Gaels.

It seems clear now that the Ordnance Survey mappers who travelled around Argyll in the 1860s put the 'h' into 'Rinns' mainly to make it look more exotic. In the case of the island of Rhum/Rum it is thought that they put in the extra letter to avoid offending Victorian sensibilities regarding alcoholic drinks popular with the working class. Today all this seems patronising.

So although almost everybody in Islay has got used to the 'Rhinns', and although this spelling was used before them by their fathers and grandfathers, before *that*, if it was ever written down, it was the 'Rinns'. What would be best of all would be if future generations of islanders called it by its Gaelic name!

The gleaming houses of Port Charlotte, with the backdrop of Beinn Tart a' Mhill (photo: Norman Newton)

6 STANDING STONES IN AN ORWELLIAN ENVIRONMENT

THE ISLAND OF JURA (Norse 'Dyr-ey', deer-island) lies to the east and north of Islay. Access is via the Port Askaig – Feolin ferry, operated by Western Ferries, which makes frequent crossings carrying both vehicles and passengers. The high mountains at the south end of the island have been known as the Paps of Jura since at least the sixteenth century, and not only dominate their immediate environment but also form part of the seascape for many miles around. From Kintyre, Colonsay, Coll, Tiree and Mull, and from the high tops on the western seaboard of Scotland from Skye to Arran and even from the Isle of Man and Ben Lomond, these distinctive mountains constitute part of the distant horizon. They are formed of quartzite, and their rounded forms and scree slopes are thought to be due to frost shattering at the end of the last Ice Age. Dr John Walker of Edinburgh University carried out experiments involving atmospheric pressure on the top of Beinn an Oir in 1764. Using a Torricellian barometer he estimated its height as 2,340ft, which was only 231ft short. On the summit can also be seen the remains of an observation point manned during World War II.

The other famous feature associated with Jura is the renowned whirlpool of Corrievreckan – Corrie-Bhreacan, the cauldron of Breckan. This area of raging marine turbulence lies at the tip of Jura, between Jura and the now uninhabited island of Scarba to the north. According to Gaelic folklore, Breckan was a Viking of some importance who wished to marry a local island princess. Her father was wary of the consequences of such a union, but fearful of offending the Vikings. So he gave his consent to the marriage, on condition that Breckan should prove his skill and his manhood by anchoring his longship in the whirlpool for three days and three nights.

Breckan agreed to this, but returned to Scandinavia to consult the sages of his native land. He was advised to equip himself with three ropes: one of hemp, one of wool, and one woven from the hair of virgins – it was thought that the purity of female innocence would give it the power to resist even the force of the waves. Unfortunately, having anchored in the gulf which now bears his name, and having survived the first two nights despite the tearing of first the hemp and then the wool rope, it appears that one of the contributors to the third rope must have been less than honest in her proclamation of innocence, for the rope parted and Breckan was drowned.

In *Popular Tales of the West Highlands*, John Francis Campbell – Iain Og Ile whose monument we have already admired at Bridgend – repeats the story of the Seven Big Women of Jura, with their magical powers, and the major motifs in the tale will be familiar to folklorists: a horse, a falcon, a sword, and a fair lady.

Another of his tales concerned the Old Woman or Witch of Jura and tells of an old woman with magical powers. There was a Caileach (old woman) in Jura who had a magic ball of thread by means of which she could draw any person or thing towards her. MacPhie or (MacDuffie) of Colonsay was in her clutches, and was not allowed to leave Jura; on several occasions he tried to escape to his native Colonsay in his boat, but always the Caileach would spot him, throw the magic ball of thread into his boat, and so bring him back to shore.

Eventually MacPhie found out that the magic of the Caileach's thread could be broken, but only if it was cut by an equally magic hatchet; thus he pretended to be content with his bondage until he found the chance to steal the Caileach's magic hatchet, and then he made his escape from Jura in a small boat. When the Caileach noticed his absence, she rushed as usual to the top of Beinn a Chaolis, and hailed MacPhie:

A Mhic a Phie
A Ghaoils' thasgaidh
An d'fhag thu air a chladach mi?

Oh, MacPhie
My love and treasure
Have you left me on the strand?

She hurled the magic ball of thread into MacPhie's boat, but he cut it with the Caileach's magic hatchet and made his escape. She was distraught:

A Mhic a Phie
Charrich, granda
An d'fhag thu air a chladach mi?

Oh, MacPhie
Rough-skinned and foul
Have you left me on the strand?

In despair she slid down the mountain to the sea shore, pleading with MacPhie to return. But he would not, and the marks left by the old woman's heels as she slid down Beinn a'Chaolis can still be seen. They are called Sgriob na Cailich – the slide of the old woman; they start near the top of the hill as rocky ravines and end in a trail of boulder scree. One of the best views of the

Overleaf: Paps of Jura from near Bunnahabhainn

91

MYTHOLOGICAL TALES

The kind of mythology based on fairy-tale will be familiar to those brought up on the exploits of Greek and Roman gods. In a pre-scientific age, natural features, natural phenomena and human behaviour were often explained in this way. But since the stories address some of the most basic tribulations of the human condition, who are we to devalue them by asking awkward questions about their reality or historicity? Such questions are irrelevant and miss the point.

old woman's slide is from the summer ferry which goes to Colonsay on Wednesdays only.

In the Witch of Jura the story highlights the dilemma of an ageing woman who thinks that she has her man for life, when he has secretly been longing for years to escape from the relationship without knowing how this can be done. Finally he 'cuts the thread', leaving the relationship and in this case his long-time mate, so that she is literally and symbolically 'washed up' on the shores of the ocean of life.

Truly there are many layers to these stories, and how much more meaningful they are when the teller can point to the scars on the mountainside left by the Caileach's heels! The Paps of Jura, habitat of women with magical powers, and Corrievreckan, palpable proof of the awesome power of raw nature with associated folklore, hint at the possibility of some cult or religious centre in Jura, whose reality is now blurred by the mists of pre-Christian and possibly even prehistoric antiquity. A weird piece of circumstantial evidence comes from the classical geographer Strabo who says that Poseidonius mentioned an island near Britain 'where rites are performed like those in Samothrace concerned with Demeter and Kore'. Kore is Persephone, the Greek goddess of nature and growth. Plutarch records a statement by Demetrius of Tarsus that among the Western Isles of Scotland was one 'in which Cronos was held asleep under guard of Briareus'. Briareus was one of the Uranids, monsters with a hundred arms and fifty heads who aided Zeus against Cronos and the other Titans. He is often regarded as a sea-god, and could be seen as a Kraken-like creature inhabiting Corrievreckan; while the profile of the Paps of Jura might be seen as similar to that of a recumbent giant.

All of this raises at least the possibility that these waters were visited in classical times and that the two most important features, the distinctive mountains of Jura and the great whirlpool, were known to the Greeks and incorporated into their mythology.

Archaeology reveals a human presence on Jura as early as 7000BC, with Mesolithic sites at Lussa Wood, Lealt Bay, and elsewhere. At Lealt Bay were found stone rings only 1m wide which had been used as cooking hearths. In them archaeologists found charcoal, hazelnut shells, red ochre, tiny fragments of bone, and hundreds of tiny flint tools.

From more recent prehistoric times, standing stones are found at seven sites on Jura, suggesting that in the Bronze Age it may indeed have been a ritual centre. There is a massive single stone half a mile north of Camas an Staca farmhouse, and an interesting alignment of three stones near Knockrome at the head of the Bay of the Small Isles. There is another alignment of three stones near Sannaig farmhouse. In the burial ground of the island's Early Christian church of Cill Chaluim Chille at Tarbert there is an example of what may have been a prehistoric standing stone which has been 'Christianised' by the addition of a Latin cross on each face. Clearly there was an active Bronze Age population on Jura.

The original site of the parish church of Jura was at Cill Earnadail, Keils (Killearnadale). No trace remains of the medieval church, but several medieval grave-slabs lie in the burial ground or within the mausoleum of the Campbells of Jura, erected in 1838.

There are no castles on Jura, but just off the south coast road is Claig Castle (the Castle of the Trench) on the tiny island now known as Am Fraoch Eilean (Heather Island) but formerly called Eilean Charne (the Island of the Heap of Stones). Probably built in the fifteenth century, it occupies a commanding position of strategic importance, with extensive views up the Sound of Islay and the Sound of Jura, and of the whole of the Kintyre peninsula and the island of Gigha. The ruins consist of a small tower-house of which only the ground floor remains, and traces of an enclosing bank and ditch. The ferry from Port Askaig to Kennacraig usually passes within half a mile of this castle – closer, if the captain is seeking shelter from the occasional stiff northerly breeze.

Something of the nature of farming life in former times can be seen at Keils, where various thatched buildings of cruck-framed construction can be seen as ruins or outbuildings around the modern farm. The stackyard with its cobbled stack-stances, formerly a feature of farm life before the advent of the harvester and baler, can still be seen there.

In former times the island's main harbour was at Lagg, built in the early nineteenth century in connection with the cattle trade and the increased demand for faster postal and passenger transportation to and from the mainland. The sea crossing from Lagg in Jura to Keills in Knapdale was the normal route for cattle from the islands of Islay, Jura and Colonsay: interest in this 'overland route' from Islay to the mainland has been revived recently. The beasts from Colonsay were landed at Loch Tarbert and driven overland to Lagg, while those from Islay crossed at Feolin and were driven over a hill road. A new road was built on the island at about the same time as the harbours at Feolin and Lagg, around 1810. The handsome three-arched bridge over the Corran River near Knockrome was also built at this time.

The public road system on Jura today runs from the ferry landing at Feolin to the farmhouse at Kinuachdrach, a distance of 32^1/$_2$ miles (52km). Just over eight miles along the Jura road is Craighouse, with a pier, hotel, school, doctor, distillery, fish farm, Post Office, tearoom, village hall and Jura's only shop: it is the hub of the island's social life and commerce. The hotel organises boat trips in summer to the west side of the island and to Corrievreckan. With a flood tide and a strong wind from the west or south this stretch is classed as unnavigable, even by the Royal Navy, since turbulence is severe and currents can be up to 8.5 knots; nevertheless it is still possible for small craft to pass through safely at certain states of the tide. Local knowledge is essential, however. The safest plan is probably to avoid Corrievreckan altogether, unless in the company of somebody experienced in its vagaries and idiosyncrasies. It is possible to view the whirlpool from the

GEORGE ORWELL IN JURA

Orwell, travelling under his own name of Eric Blair, first came to Jura in September 1945, staying initially at Kinuachdrach and then at Barnhill (this being a direct translation into English of the old Gaelic name, Knockintavil). From 1946 to 1949 Orwell spent the summers at Barnhill, working on his new novel which was eventually to be published under the title 1984. Unfortunately, Orwell's health deteriorated steadily – he was suffering from tuberculosis – and early in 1949 he left Jura for the last time. He died in hospital in London on 21 January 1950 at the age of forty-six.

north shore of Jura; this involves a two-hour round trip on foot from Kinuachdrach. In ideal conditions it is even possible to hear the roar of Breckan's Cauldron from the mainland of Argyll, especially from the Craignish peninsula, about four miles away.

One who failed to follow this cautious approach was the writer George Orwell, who very nearly came to grief in Corrievreckan with his son Richard and two friends. His small boat, battered and unseaworthy was wrecked on a small rocky island, though here the stranded mariners were able to light a fire which fortunately was seen by some local lobster fishermen who came to their rescue. They were lucky to escape with a soaking.

Every summer brings its quota of pilgrims who come to see where Orwell lived and worked, and perhaps sometimes to pay their respects. The road to Barnhill is rough, with few passing places, and is unsuitable for vehicles with a low clearance; but still they come, perhaps imbuing something of Orwell's determination and persistence. They would surely all agree with Orwell's description of Barnhill: 'It's in an extremely un-getatable place!'

Since prehistoric times, human settlement has been concentrated into a narrow strip of land along the south and east coasts of the island – for the truth is that the rest of Jura is a quartzite desert, albeit very beautiful, and very wet! For the yachtsman or the visitor with plenty of time, a trip to the west coast, where the unsurpassed raised beaches can be enjoyed in total solitude, is a rewarding experience. The population of Jura has dwindled over the last 150 years from around 1,000 to fewer than 200 today, but it is a lively enough community, and well above the limits of viability for island life.

On the other hand there are 5,000 red deer on Jura, so it is still living up to its Norse name. Depending on your position in the social hierarchy, they are either a blessing or a curse: to the rich and to the estate owners (to be fair, not always the same thing!), Jura's barren quartzite wilderness is dignified by the designation of 'deer forest', now a rather quaint term describing areas which are equally dangerous for hill-walkers and red deer stags. George Orwell, and other incomers sympathetic to the islanders' needs and aspirations, saw deer as the curse of the island, a point of view with which the hard-pressed officers of the Forestry Commission would agree, since deer just love young conifers.

7 BIRDS, ROCKS AND RUINS:
WALKS AND EXCURSIONS

ACCESS

BEFORE DESCRIBING some of the possible walking excursions on Islay and Jura, a brief word about access. Basically access to the country-side in Islay, and to all historic sites, is unrestricted, bounded only by considerations of courtesy and common sense. It is sensible to ask for directions, if not for permission. Any advice offered should be followed, and visitors should take particular care not to damage dykes and fences, and to avoid disturbing stock, especially in the lambing season.

Freedom of access does not give visitors the right to tamper with historic sites without the owner's permission. Similarly, even though Islay's hill lochs are well stocked with brown trout, visitors must apply to the appropriate estate for permits to fish. Hotels and the Tourist Information Centre can offer advice about where to apply: on some lochs boats are available. The same applies to anybody wishing to fish for salmon or to shoot game. Doing these things without permission is poaching, and is illegal.

Fields near Sunderland Farm with Loch Gorm on the left

So, although there are no laws prohibiting rights of access, there has to be some give and take with landowners and farmers since it is their livelihood which is often at stake, as well as other people's jobs. And from the point of view of personal safety it is reckless to go hill-walking on big shooting estates during the shooting season. Again, the estate offices can advise if any shooting parties are likely to be on the hills.

EQUIPMENT

VISITORS ALWAYS HOPE for good weather, but in our climate there are no guarantees, only wishful thinking, and in the absence of a direct line to the Almighty certain precautions are essential. The key elements in Islay's weather are wetness and wind. Even when the sky is blue and the lochs are shimmering with scenic beauty, the ground underfoot is likely to be boggy once off roads and tracks. Adequate rain-gear and correct footwear will make it possible to have a good time, whatever the weather; inadequate protection leads inevitably to saturation, cold, misery, recriminations and regret. Wet clothing can be dried out – eventually – but without doubt prevention is better. Even on a fine day there is likely to be a brisk breeze, and light, windproof jackets or anoraks should always be carried. The weather can change quickly, and although inadequately clad walkers are unlikely to come to any harm in these gentle landscapes, they can certainly become exceedingly miserable very quickly.

Correct footwear is most important. Proper walking boots with Vibram soles are best, and need not be expensive or heavy; good walking shoes are acceptable only for farm tracks or beachcombing expeditions. Trainers will become soaked in anything but drought conditions and can be ruined quickly and easily; Wellies are uncomfortable to walk in for any distance, and are positively dangerous in wet conditions. If you buy new boots or shoes for your island adventure, try to break them in first, or come well provided with plasters to deal with the inevitable blisters.

KILCHIARAN TO KILCHOMAN
2–3 HOURS

FROM PORT CHARLOTTE or Portnahaven drive to Kilchiaran Farm. Take the first track on the right, which leads up towards the radio masts. You can park your car at the gate, though make sure that you don't block access to the fields for the farmer.

Once through the gate, the track forks. Take the left branch which leads down and round Rubha na h Airde Moire, the point of the big headland. The track is well formed – it was once an old drove road. Follow

Right: Monument in the cemetery at Kilchoman

it down towards the beach, and perhaps detour to have a look at Dun Chroisprig (Norse 'kross-borg' – 'the fort of the cross'), an Iron Age fort in front of the cliffs to the east. This is a 'galleried' dun, showing some of the features of a broch in that the drystone wall has a hollow or gallery built into it. At one point the surviving stonework is 1.1m (3.5ft) high, in five courses. The wall is 3.5m (11ft) thick on average, enclosing an internal diameter of 12m (40ft). An outer wall provided added defence.

Nearer the sea on your left is another, smaller dun. Continue down to the beach, and walk along it until you come to a burn, then take the right-hand track leading up to the houses, and turn right there. Past the former coastguard cottages just before the next houses, go through a gate into the field, and make your way to the Commonwealth War Memorial and graves. Then, continue on to Kilchoman church, built in 1825 but now abandoned and in an unstable condition. In the burial ground are medieval grave-slabs, and the famous Kilchoman cross, a masterpiece of medieval stone carving. Return to Kilchiaran.

You are likely to see choughs, one of Britain's rarest breeding birds, at any point on this walk. The cliffs on your right, now far inland, were made by the sea when the sea-level was higher, at the end of the last Ice Age.

BALLYGRANT TO BALEACHDRACH
2¹/₂ HOURS

FROM BALLYGRANT VILLAGE take the road marked Mulindry. After about half a mile take the turning on the left. Continue up the hill and at a clearing in the woods to the left of the road stop to enjoy the views of Ballygrant Loch and its surrounding woodland, with the Paps of Jura behind. Look for the crannog (artificial island) in the loch, dating probably to the Iron Age. You are on the Lossit estate: continue on the estate road past Lossit kennels and Lossit Lodge. The road rises above the woodland into open country overlooking Lossit Loch, with another crannog. Continue to Lossit Farm, through the farmyard and on to a farm track, still heading east. From the high point of the track pause to enjoy the views of the Sound of Islay, Jura, Kintyre and Arran.

At this point those with an interest in antiquities will be rewarded by heading up the hill to the left, to the north of the track, to Dun Bhoraraig, an Iron Age broch, now ruinous but once a stone tower which in 100BC may have stood 13m (43ft) high. Rejoin the farm track after pausing to enjoy the panoramic view, which ranges from Mull to Arran on a clear day.

Follow the track, which now starts downhill, down through woodland until it reaches a barn, which makes an ideal spot for a picnic and a breather. More energetic walkers may wish to walk on down the hill to the sea.

Return to Ballygrant.

Left: Lossit Bay

Overleaf: Looking south-west from near Dun Bhoraraig

101

ARDTALLA TO PROAIG
2¹/₂ HOURS

THIS IS A FAIRLY EASY WALK along a well-defined track, but unless it hasn't rained in Islay for the last six weeks – it does happen from time to time! – you should be prepared to get your feet wet as the track gets waterlogged at several places, and there are three streams to cross.

The walk starts at Ardtalla, past Kildalton. Until the 1950s the track was used by a horse and cart regularly, and it still takes four-wheel-drive vehicles delivering shooting parties into the hills. Behind the house at Ardtalla go through a gate into a field; follow the track to the north-east, and go through another gate. Take care to close all gates firmly behind you, and avoid upsetting the stock. The track now turns northwards. About half a mile north of Ardtalla a new fence crosses the old track; look for the stile to cross it.

About a mile north of Ardtalla the Iron Age fort of Dun na Gall – the Fort of the Strangers – occupies a promontory. The track proceeds northwards overlooking the Sound of Islay, looking across to Jura. As it drops

down to the valley of the River Proaig you are walking on a raised beach; now it is high and dry, but 10,000 years ago the sea-level at the end of the last Ice Age was higher than it is now. The ground around Proaig is obviously greener, a sign of the fertility that made this an attractive homestead to Viking settlers who gave the place its name: Proaig means 'broad bay' in the Old Norse language. In the Middle Ages it was one of the most prosperous and prestigious farms on Islay, and was occupied by the family of the Lords of the Isles, the MacDonald chiefs who ruled the Hebrides from the 1150s until 1493. Their descendants continued there long afterwards, and successive houses were built at Proaig right up to the nineteenth century. The last farmhouse and its steadings are now derelict, having been abandoned in the 1930s. The last generation of children brought up there, now in their sixties, walked

Left: Peat stack on the Oa

to school every day to Ardmore, two miles south of Ardtalla. The house with the bell tower was Ardmore School.

Proaig is a wonderful place to explore for traces of old houses, to picnic, or to watch for otters, before returning to Ardtalla. Off to the north-east is the lighthouse on MacArthur's Head; to the north-west a very rough and difficult track – for experienced walkers only – leads through the hills for ten very demanding miles to Storakaig. This is very wild and remote country, and not to be attempted without a map, a compass, and proper gear.

BEACHES

AMONG THE GREAT ATTRACTIONS for holidaymakers in Islay are the many totally unspoilt beaches, but a word of caution is necessary as some of them are extremely dangerous for bathing. The safe beaches are in the sheltered waters of Loch Gruinart and Loch Indaal. At Tayvulin near Ardnave Farm and on the east side of Ardnave Point and at Killinallan there are sandy beaches with safe bathing, and seals basking on the tidal flats are an added attraction.

Laggan Bay in Loch Indaal has nearly 8 miles (12km) of continuous sandy beach stretching from Kintra in the south to Laggan Point in the north. At the head of Loch Indaal there is safe bathing, with the area near Black Rock a good, sheltered picnic spot. There are several good sandy beaches on the Kildalton road, for example at Ardtalla, Ardilistry and Aros. On the other side of Loch Indaal there are safe beaches at Port Charlotte, and at Port Bhain, at the monument between Bruichladdich and Port Charlotte.

On the other hand the beaches on the west coast of Islay, although sandy and spectacular, are dangerous and not suitable for swimming. This is particularly true of the beaches at Kilchoman, Saligo and Sanaigmore, which are all easily accessible by car and ideal for picnicking – but not for swimming! There are of course many other beaches around the shores of Islay which have not been mentioned here. Part of the fun of visiting Islay is to find your own favourite spots, possibly involving only a short walk from the more popular beaches. Not that they are ever crowded by the standards of Blackpool or Bournemouth – to the locals a beach is crowded if there are half-a-dozen people on a mile-long stretch of sand!

The safety factor cannot be emphasised too strongly. Conditions can change at any of the beaches from one day to the next, depending on the wind and the tide.

Machir Bay

Overleaf: Laggan Bay from the south end

USEFUL INFORMATION AND PLACES TO VISIT

TOURIST INFORMATION

Tourist Information Centre, The Square, Bowmore
Accommodation, leaflets, books, maps. Tel: 01496 810254.

FERRY SERVICES

Caledonian MacBrayne, Kennacraig.
Tel: 01880 730253.

Caledonian MacBrayne, Port Ellen.
Tel: 01496 302209.

Glenegedale Airport.
Tel: 01496 302022.

Western Ferries, The Pier, Port Askaig.
Jura ferry. Tel: 01496 840681.

PLACES TO VISIT

Bowmore Distillery
Open all year. Tours – weekdays only from 10.00am. Saturday morning tour at 10.30am, May–Sept. Free guiding and tasting. Facilities for disabled. Gift shop. Tel: 01496 810441.

Caol Ila Distillery and Visitor Centre
Open all year. Free guided tour and tasting, Mon–Fri by appointment only. Gift shop. Tel: 01496 840207.

Carraig Fhada Lighthouse
Crafts, knitwear, singing sands and beach walks. Tel: 01496 302114.

C. & E. Roy, The Celtic House, Bowmore
Excellent bookshop, crafts, gifts. Tel: 01496 810304

Dunivaig Castle, Lagavulin
Ruins of medieval castle on top of the earlier fortress of the MacDonald Lords of the Isles. Dangerous stonework – keep well clear.

Elizabeth Sykes Batiks, Port Charlotte
Original pictures, scarves, etc, hand-dyed. Open daily. Tel: 01496 850357.

Finlaggan Visitor Centre, Finlaggan Cottage
Open April, Thurs and Sun, 2.30pm–5.00pm; May–Sept, Tues, Thurs and Sun, 2.30pm–5.00pm; Oct, Sundays only, 2.00pm–4.00pm or by arrangement.
Guided tours of islands while excavations are in progress. Administrative complex of the medieval Lords of the Isles: ruined buildings, graveslabs, chapel. Tel: 01496 850273.

Islay Celtic Craft Shop & Gallery, Main Street, Bowmore
Original paintings and gift shop.
Tel: 01496 810262.

Islay Field Centre, Port Charlotte
Open daily, April–October. Displays and exhibitions of Islay's wildlife, slide shows, children's corner, quizzes.
Tel: 01496 850288.

Islay Lifeboat Station, Port Askaig
Open Thurs, May–Sept, 2.00pm–4.00pm. Souvenirs on sale for RNLI.

Islay Woollen Mill Co. Ltd, Bridgend
Industrial archaeology, gift shop. Tel: 01496 810563.

Kildalton Cross and Old Parish Church
Magnificent Early Christian carved wheel-cross, medieval stone effigy of warrior, medieval chapel.

Kintra Outdoor Centre, Kintra Farm
Restaurant, accommodation, including hostel, caravan and camping. Tel: 01496 302051.

Lagavulin Distillery and Visitor Centre
Open all year. Free guided tour and tasting, Mon–Fri, 9.30am–5pm. Tel: 01496 302250.

Loch Gruinart Nature Reserve, Aoradh Farm
Visitor Centre open daily, 10.00am–5.00pm. Farm visits, guided walks, displays, 4,000 acres (1,667ha) run by RSPB.
Tel: 01496 850505.

MacTaggart Pool, Bowmore
Open Tues–Fri, 12.30pm–8.30pm; Sat–Sun, 10.30am–5.30pm. 25m pool, sauna, sunbed, launderette, swimming classes. Tel: 01496 810767.

Museum of Islay Life, Port Charlotte
Open daily, Easter–October, Sunday afternoons, and by appointment. Award-winning displays of archaeology and island life. Library and archive, including photographs.
Tel: 01496 850358.

Port Ellen Pottery, Tighcargaman, Port Ellen
Pottery handmade on the premises. Tel: 01496 302345.

Round Church, Bowmore
Built in 1767 – no corners for the Devil to hide in. Monuments to the Campbell of Shawfield lairds.

PLACE-NAMES AND THEIR PRONUNCIATION

The place-names of Islay and Jura constitute a record of human settlement on the islands over thousands of years. Gaelic-speaking people first came to Islay from the coast of Antrim, in Ireland, soon after AD300, although there were no doubt frequent contacts before that. The Romans called the tribes of Ireland *Scoti*, and they became known as 'Scots' in their new lands. They spread over the whole island of Islay and the rest of what is now Argyll, and established a kingdom which became known as Dalriada. In AD843 the King of Dalriada, Kenneth MacAlpine, married a Pictish princess and became the united ruler of the Picts and the Scots – the first king of what is now call Scotland.

But soon after AD800 Viking raiders appeared on the west coasts, soon to be followed by waves of Norse settlers. For three hundred and fifty years Islay was densely occupied by this new population, which inter-married with the locals and left its mark on the landscape in many farm names – for example all the names ending in *-bus* or *-bolls* are derived from the Norse *-bolstadr*, a farmstead.

The *kil-* names of Islay and Jura date from two hundred and fifty years before the Vikings came, when Early Christian saints, mostly Irish, established churches and monasteries throughout the Gaelic-speaking colonies.

Ardnave	G. *àird an naoimh*	Ard-*nave*	the saint's point
Ballinaby	G. *Bail' an aba*	Balin-*a*-bee	the abbot's farm
Ballygrant	G. *Bail' a' ghràna*	Ba-lee-*grant*	the grain township
Bowmore	G. *am Bodha mór*	Bow-*more*	the big reef
Bruichladdich	G. *Bruthach-cladach*	Broo-ich-*lad*-ee	brae of the shore
Bunnahabhainn	G. *Bun na h-abhann*	Boo-na-*ha*-ven	river mouth
Caol Ila	G. *caol Ila*	*Col-ee*-la	sound of Islay
Carrabus	N. *kjarr + bolstadr*	*Car*-a-bus	copse farm
Carrag Fhada	G. *carraig fhada*	Ca-rick-*fa*-ta	the long sea rock
Conisby	N. *konr + by*	*Con*-is-bee	the king's estate
Cornabus	N. *korn + bolstadr*	*Corn*-a-bus	corn farm
Dun Nosebridge	N. *knaus borg*	*Nose*-bridge	crag fort
Eallabus	N. *Olaf + bolstadr*	*Yall*-a-bus	Oli's farm
Finlaggan	G. *fionn laggan*	Fin-*la*-gan	an Irish saint
Jura	N. *dyr + ey*	Due-ra	deer island
Kilchiaran	G. *cill Chiarain*	Kil-*chee*-ran	St Ciaran's church
Kilchoman	G. *cill Chommain*	Kil-*cho*-man	St Comman's church
(St Comman was the brother of Cuimein, seventh abbot of Iona, 657–669)			
Killinallan	G. *cill an àilein*	Kil-in-*al*-in	church on the green meadow

Killarow	G. *cill Mhaelrubha*	Kil-a-*roo*	St Maelrubha
Kilnave	G. *cill naoimh*	Kil-*nave*	church of the saints
Lagavulin	G. *lag a' mhuilinn*	Lag-a-*vool*-in	mill hollow
Octofad	G. *ochdamh fada*	Oct-o-*fad*	long eighth farm
Octomore	G. *ochdamh mòr*	Oct-o-*more*	big eighth farm

(the 'octave' was an ancient land measure, being one-eighth of a 'davoch', which was equal to twenty 'pennylands')

Persabus	N. *pearsa*	*Per*-sa-bus	the priest's farm
Port Askaig	N. *askr + vik*	*Ass*-kaig	port of the ash-wooded bay
Port Charlotte			after a laird's mother
Port Ellen			after a laird's wife
Portnahaven	G. *port na h-abhann*	Port-na-*hay*-van	the river port
Rubh'a'mhaill	G. *rubha a'mhail*	Roo-a-*val*	rough promontory
Uiskentuie	G. *uisge an t-suidhe*	Oosh-ken-*too*-ee	water of the resting place

G. – Gaelic
N. – Norse

FURTHER READING

Gillies, H. Cameron. *The Place-names of Argyll* (Nutt, 1906)

Jupp, Clifford. *History of Islay* (Museum of Islay Life, 1994)

Lamont, W. D. *The Early History of Islay* (1966)

Newton, Norman S. *Islay* (David & Charles, 1988)

Royal Commission on the Ancient and Historical Monuments of Scotland. *Argyll: an inventory of the monuments*, vol. 5 – *Islay, Jura, Colonsay and Oronsay* (HMS0, 1984)

Smith, G. Gregory (ed.). *The Book of Islay: Documents Illustrating the History of the Island* (1895)

The Stent Book and Acts of the Bailiary of Islay, 1718–1843 (1890)

Steer, Kenneth A. and Bannerman, John. *Late Medieval Sculpture in the West Highlands* (HMSO, 1977)

Storrie, Margaret C. *Islay: Biography of an Island* (Oa Press, 1981)

Welsh, Mary. *Walks on Islay* (Westmoreland Gazette, 1996)

Wilson, Neil. *Scotch and Water: an Illustrated Guide to the Hebridean Malt Whisky Distilleries* (Lochar Publishing, 1985)

INDEX

Page numbers in *italic* indicate illustrations